D0806844

General Editor:
Patrick McNeill

SOCIETY
NOW

Social Class and Stratification

Other books in the **Society Now** series

Peter Saunders

SOCIAL CLASS AND STRATIFICATION

London and New York

First published 1990
by Routledge
11 New Fetter Lane, London EC4P 4EE

Simultaneously published in the USA and Canada
by Routledge
a division of Routledge, Chapman and Hall, Inc.
29 West 35th Street, New York, NY 10001

Reprinted 1992

© 1990 Peter Saunders

Set by Hope Services, Abingdon
Printed and bound in Great Britain by
The Guernsey Press Co. Ltd., Guernsey, Channel Islands

British Library Cataloguing in Publication Data

Saunders, Peter 1950–
Social class and stratification (Society now)
1. Great Britain. Social class
I. Title II. Series
305.5′0941

ISBN 0–415–04125–2

Contents

Preface

Sociology in Britain today is strongly underpinned by a left-wing political consensus – what I have termed elsewhere a 'socialist–feminist orthodoxy'. This bias appears to be particularly marked in GCE A-level texts, as Professor David Marsland's recent book, *Seeds of Bankruptcy* (1988), London and Lexington: Claridge Press, all too depressingly demonstrates.

Too often in contemporary sociology, opinion is allowed to substitute for analysis and socialist values are adopted uncritically as the starting point of commentary and evaluation. The analysis of social class and inequality is peculiarly susceptible to this problem, given the centrality of these issues to socialist theory and politics. Social stratification is one of the most crucial and fascinating areas of contemporary sociology, but it is also one of the areas where science and politics have become dangerously entangled.

It is often said that all sociological accounts are partial. This is true. But this does not mean that we have to neglect competing explanations which do not agree with our own, nor does it mean that we can ignore empirical evidence which does not say what we want it to say.

In this book I have tried to present for the student a range of perspectives and to evaluate them against the available evidence. I have made a particular effort to include material drawn from the neo-liberal tradition (the so-called 'New Right'), for what passes for debate in the sociology of stratification has generally ignored this literature altogether. My aim has been to produce a book which goes some way to meet David Marsland's demand for 'genuinely open debate' within the A-level sociology syllabus.

I would like to thank David Marsland for initially stimulating me to write this book, Pete Langley for encouraging me to publish it in this form, and Pat McNeill for his helpful comments on an earlier draft.

1

Marx, Weber, and social stratification

The concept of 'social stratification'

The term 'stratification' has been borrowed by sociologists from the science of geology. There it refers to the successive layers or strata of rock and other materials which have been laid down over the millennia to form the earth's crust. Translated into the very different science of sociology, the concept of stratification has been adapted to refer to the different 'layers' or strata of social groups which are thought to be arranged, one on top of the other, in various human societies. Thus, just as the geologist who drives a bore-hole into the earth may discover a layer of sandstone on top of a layer of basalt on top of a layer of granite, so too the sociologist who digs deep down into the social structure may discover layer upon layer of different kinds of social groupings – upper classes upon middle classes upon lower classes, for example.

The study of social stratification is the study of how these different groupings or strata relate to one another. Usually we find that they are related unequally. One group may own and enjoy more economic resources than another, or it may be held in higher esteem, or it may be in a position to order other groups around. In our own society there are poor and wealthy people, there are families of high birth and families of commoners, and there are politically powerful elites and relatively powerless groups of people who are expected only to follow commands and obey orders. The analysis of social stratification is concerned to understand how inequalities like these arise in the first place, how they are maintained or changed over time, and the impact which they have on other aspects of social life.

There are, of course, different ways in which groups may be stratified. In most societies, for example, there are clear systems of stratification based on gender. Inequalities between men and women may be found in the kinds of work they do, the opportunities which are open to them, the chance to become powerful leaders, and so on. Similarly, it is common to discover systems of stratification which operate between different racial or ethnic groups. Sometimes one ethnic group enslaves another; sometimes one excludes another from economic privileges and political rights; and so on. It may also be possible to identify stratification operating on the basis of age, religion or caste.

In this study, however, we shall not pay much attention to these aspects of social stratification. The issues raised by gender and generational inequalities have already been discussed in other books in this series (O'Donnell 1985 and Garrett 1987) and these should be consulted as complementary sources. In this book, our principal concern will be with that specific aspect of social stratification which has to do with the relationship between social classes.

Before considering how sociologists have tried to analyse class stratification, we should first take note of the limitations of using the term 'stratification' at all. Sociology has often made use of ideas derived from other sciences – the so-called 'organic analogy' in which human societies are likened to living organisms is the best-known example. But such parallels are always limited and can be misleading. In the case of the stratification metaphor, for example, it is obvious that the arrangement of different social groups within a society is not really like the arrangements of rock in the earth's crust. Geological strata do not interact with one another, for example, whereas in even the most rigid and hierarchical of societies there is some degree of interaction between groups at the top and those at the bottom. Similarly, different geological layers cannot change places relative to one another whereas in human societies, one group may 'rise' in power and status over time while another group may 'fall'. Fifty years ago in Britain, for example, clerks were undoubtedly more highly esteemed than they are today. Similarly, in the USA, it is possible to observe the 'rise' in status of different ethnic groups such as the Italians or the Poles who previously occupied very lowly positions as recent immigrants to that society. And in many Western societies, the position of women relative to that of men has been changing somewhat over the last twenty years or so.

Not only do social groups rise and fall relative to one another, but so too do individual members of these groups. One of the main problems with employing the metaphor of stratification within sociology is precisely that it cannot capture the idea of individual movement between levels. The notion of individual bits of granite or limestone or whatever moving up and down within the earth's crust is absurd, yet most human societies have enabled some degree of individual movement between strata. This is true (though far from common) of even the most repressive of social systems. Slaves in ancient Rome could very occasionally become free citizens, and serfs in medieval Europe who managed to escape and evade capture for a year and a day could throw off their bondage and become 'free men'. In modern industrial countries, such movement is much more common. In the Soviet Union, where power and status very often depend upon position in the Communist Party hierarchy, it is quite common to find children of peasant and working-class families rising to high political office (see, for example, Lane 1971). And in Western capitalist countries, movement both up and down between different social classes is remarkably common, as we shall see later in this chapter.

These and other examples of what sociologists term *individual social mobility* have no real parallel in geology, and to this extent, the idea of a system of stratification composed of solid and immutable layers of different composition seems highly misleading when applied to the analysis of most contemporary human societies.

Activities

1 For each of the following societies, try to decide if there is any *one* characteristic − age, class, gender, ethnicity, nationality, religion, etc. − which is more important than any other in shaping people's life chances:
    Northern Ireland
    The Soviet Union
    Israel
    The Deep South of the USA
    The United Arab Emirates
    South Africa
    Rural provinces of India

2 Try to rank each of the following characteristics in terms of their importance in shaping economic inequalities in contemporary Britain:
    The job people do
    Their gender
    Their ethnic identity
    The family they are born into
    The region of the country they live in
    Their religious affiliation
    How old they are

Which are the least and which are the most important factors in shaping social stratification in Britain today? How have these changed over the last 200 years?

═══════════════════════════════════════

Marx on the bourgeoisie and the proletariat

Why, if it is so misleading, has the metaphor of social stratification become so pervasive in modern sociology? One answer probably lies in the influence of Marxist theory within this branch of the discipline, for Marxism is much more concerned with the different strata than it is with the individuals within them.

Karl Marx was a nineteenth-century theorist who developed his key ideas about the class structure of modern societies in the forty years following the wave of European revolutions in 1848. It seemed to him that he was witnessing the emergence of a modern age in which the division between two great social classes was destined to become the central feature.

As Marx saw it, all societies that had ever existed had been 'class societies' of one kind or another. There was in his view one overriding principle governing the organisation of human affairs in all societies up to and including the advent of capitalism, and that was that one section of the population owned and controlled the basic material resources at the society's disposal while another section owned nothing. In ancient Rome, for example, one group owned the land while another was forced to work as slaves in order to get the subsistence (mainly food and shelter) required to live. Similarly, in feudal Europe, the lords owned all the land and the serfs were obliged to perform labour and military duties for the lords in return for access to a strip of land which they could farm for themselves. And in capitalism too, according to Marx, one group of people (the bourgeoisie or capitalist class) owns the factories, land and banks while another (the proletariat) has no choice but to work for the capitalists in return for a subsistence wage which never reflects the real value of what is produced in the course of labour. In all of these societies, therefore, the class which owns the means of production grows ever wealthier by exploiting the labour of the class which owns nothing. Just as the slaves and the serfs of earlier periods created the wealth which was then taken from them, so too in capitalism, wage labourers are obliged to create the goods and services which their employers then take and sell, retaining the proceeds for themselves.

Marx did not deny that sometimes workers could become capitalists – it is in principle possible for a worker to borrow or accumulate a small sum of capital, invest it in a business, succeed in marketing the products and eventually expand to a point where he or she begins to employ other workers. Marx was also aware that capitalists could become workers – indeed, his theory held that over time, more and more capitalists would see their businesses fail and would therefore 'descend' into the ranks of the proletariat. But although he recognised the possibility of such upward and downward social mobility, Marx did not consider it to be very important (nor, in the case of upward mobility, very likely).

Much more important for Marx was the existence of these two social classes as the basic and essential elements of society conceived as a system of production. In other words, the fact that a few individuals might 'make good' or fail was irrelevant to the continuing existence of a system which required that there always be two classes, one owning the basic productive resources of the society, and the other obliged to work in order to live. It did not really matter which individuals found themselves in which of these classes, for his focus was on the system, not on the individuals within it. Capitalists as individuals might be morally good or bad people, and some of them might even deplore the poverty to which their workers were consigned – in Britain, for example, there were many instances during the eighteenth and nineteenth centuries of bourgeois families who tried to improve the lot of their workers by setting up schools for their children, establishing model communities for them to live in, and so on. For Marx, however, the essential point was that in the end, such people would still have to operate according to the logic of the capitalist system of which they were a part. If a capitalist insisted on paying higher wages, or reducing the hours of work, or improving working and home conditions, he or she would simply be undercut by competitors and would eventually go out of business.

Seen in this way, the only change or movement which mattered in society was one which would shatter the system itself by means of a revolutionary upheaval. Just as an earthquake or volcanic eruption fundamentally reorders the stratified layers of rock and sediment beneath the earth's surface by bringing to the top boiling rock which has hitherto been compressed far below, so too revolutions break up existing social orders and bring to the top new classes which have hitherto been repressed and contained. For Marx, piecemeal reform can never change very much, and there is precious little which individuals on their own can do to make things any different. If, implausibly, a worker does manage to start a successful business and grow to become a major capitalist entrepreneur, this only means that some other capitalist loses profits and goes bust. If the system stays the same, then the domination of one class by another also stays the same, no matter how much the composition of those classes might change. Individual movement up and down the system thus does nothing to change it – which is why, from a Marxist point of view, the geological metaphor of stratified layers in society seems so appropriate.

Exploitation as the basis of class struggle

It follows from all of this that the Marxist view of social stratification is one which sees classes as *real and objective entities*. A social class is much more than the sum of the individuals who comprise it, for these individuals are all obliged by the logic of the system to act in much the same

7

way, and they will also tend to think in much the same way too. All capitalists *must* try to accumulate capital by paying the lowest wages they can, by increasing the efficiency of the productive process wherever possible, and by selling at the maximum price they can attain. Similarly, all workers *must* sell their labour-power if they want to live, and must in the process keep contributing to the growing wealth and power of the class which is oppressing them. If everybody had access to the means of production – the land, tools, factories and so on – then they would get back the full value of the labour they put into production. Somebody who worked for eight hours to produce, say, a knitted jumper would be able to exchange it for goods and services made up of eight hours of other people's labour time. Nobody, in other words, would be exploited. But in a situation where one class monopolises access to means of production, it is in a position to give back to workers less than the full value of their labour. Thus, the person who has to go and knit jumpers in a factory for eight hours receives back, not the value of the goods he or she has made, but rather a wage which is only sufficient to buy the essential things necessary for him or her to stay alive and hence to turn up for work again the following morning. The difference between the value of the jumpers produced, and the value of the wage received, is what is taken by the factory owner as profit.

According to Marx, this means that exploitation is an objective fact of life in capitalist systems, just as it was in feudal and slave societies. And just as, even if Roman slaves insisted that they were quite happy with things as they were and felt that they were getting a fair deal, this would do nothing to change the objective fact of their exploitation, so too in capitalist societies, evidence of worker happiness, contentment or even active support for the system does nothing to alter the fact that they are members of an oppressed and exploited class whose long-term interests lie in the overthrow of that system.

This insistence in Marx's theory on the objective character

8

of class relations and exploitation is crucial, for it means that the theory can still claim to be correct even when ordinary working-class people reject it. Engels, a wealthy Manchester factory owner who collaborated with Marx through much of his life, coined the term 'false consciousness' to refer precisely to the situation where the working class failed to understand its 'true' and 'objective' situation as an oppressed class whose lot could only be improved by the overthrow of the capitalist system. Indeed, Marx and Engels built into their theory an explanation of why workers very often did not and could not appreciate their true predicament, for they argued that in any society, the class that owns the means of production also tends directly or indirectly to control the dominant ideas which are current in that society. In other words, we all the time tend to see our world through the distorting mirror of ruling class *ideology*. This argument has subsequently been taken up and embellished by later Marxist writers such as the Hungarian, Georg Lukács, who tried to show that left to its own devices, the working class would never fully understand the necessity of liberating itself through a socialist revolution, and that it therefore needed to be led by socialist intellectuals. Much the same idea can be found in Lenin's writings on the need for a revolutionary 'vanguard party' to lead the proletariat to socialism, just as it can in Antonio Gramsci's writings on 'hegemony' and Louis Althusser's concept of 'ideological state apparatuses'.

The essential point shared by all these writers is that everyday life in capitalist societies obscures the reality of the system of exploitation. In part, this is because the newspapers and electronic media, together with the schools and other agencies, reproduce the ideas of the dominant class as if they were obvious, natural and common-sense. But it is also because the process of exploitation itself is not obvious in the way that it was under slavery or feudalism. The slave who worked all day for a subsistence meal, and the serf who tilled the lord's land in order to be given a strip of land for his own use, could see that the product of their labour was being taken from them, but this is not the case with the modern worker. What seems to happen under capitalism is a free and equal exchange of so many hours' work for so many pounds in the wage packet. The fact that the wage is less than the value of what the worker has produced may not be apparent to either party, and so it is that exploitation goes unnoticed.

For Marx, then, capitalism is a system of class domination. There are two main classes which are locked together in an unequal relation of power and exploitation. Obviously, the dominant class is wealthier and enjoys a better quality of life than the subordinate class, but this is not the essential difference between them, for the basic issue has to do with who owns the means of production rather than the subsequent distribution of the goods and services which come to be produced. In some circumstances, for example at times of expansion when labour may be in short supply, wages may rise and workers may consider themselves quite well off, but this does nothing to change the facts of class exploitation and oppression which are grounded in the system of ownership. Nor does it matter if working-class people do not think of themselves as working-class, for this is not a matter of subjective judgement. Like it or not, recognise it or not, we live in a class society, and the basic mode of social organisation will not change until capitalism is overthrown and replaced by a socialist system in which the means of production are owned in common.

Problems in the Marxist approach

Marx's ideas have been enormously influential in Western sociological thinking about class, especially since the 1960s when the growth of student unrest and the first signs that the long post-war economic boom was ending combined to reawaken sociological interest in Marxist theory. Yet the problems with this whole mode of analysis are manifold.

Not all societies are class societies

First, it is not true that all human societies have been class societies. For Marx, the structuring principle of all social systems ever since the early pastoralists settled on the land has been the division between a class of owners and a class of non-owners. Yet the division between those who own the means of production (normally land) and those who do not has not always been the key to understanding social structures. In some tribal societies, the basic social divisions are drawn on the basis of age and gender, not class. In these societies, the organisation of work is often rigidly determined by gender – women may tend cattle and cook food while men hunt and fight. Similarly, lines of authority may be drawn on the basis of gender and age as responsibility for making collectively binding decisions and judgements is reserved to groups such as the male elders.

Similarly, in the traditional life of rural India, the fundamental social cleavages are structured not around class relations of ownership and non-ownership, but around divisions between castes. People's caste membership is fixed at birth and the opportunities and responsibilities open to them are rigidly determined by their caste. Thus, for example, caste governs all forms of social interaction and regulates the range of eligible partners at marriage. Castes may not eat in each other's presence lest higher caste members become 'polluted' through exposure to people of a lower caste, and there are prohibitions on the kind of food which particular castes may eat. Occupations too are reserved in such a way that what are considered to be 'ritually polluting' tasks such as the cutting of hair or the slaughter of animals may only be performed by the lowest strata – the 'untouchables'. What is important about all this is that members of a high caste may be no better off materially than their social inferiors – in Marxist terms, they may all be peasants scratching a living on their own small plots of land. To analyse such a stratification system in

Marxist class terminology is simply to misunderstand the way in which the society is structured and organised.

Even feudal Europe does not readily lend itself to Marxist class analysis. Certainly it is true that in medieval times, the lords owned the land and the serfs had to work unpaid in order to achieve access to a strip of land which they could cultivate for their own needs. But this society was ordered by the relations between 'estates', each with its own specified rights and duties, rather than by ownership of productive resources as such. In France, for example, the population was divided into nobility, clergy and the 'third estate' (mainly professionals and merchants) each of which was represented in the Assembly of the 'Estates General'. Similarly, in Britain there was a division between 'Lords' and 'Commons'. These divisions were based more on social factors, such as high birth, than on economic ownership. An aristocrat remained an aristocrat irrespective of the resources at his disposal (women, of course, were excluded from ownership altogether). The deep cleavages and conflicts in society at this time were not generally those between owners and non-owners, but those between the King and the nobles or the Church, or between different lineages, or between the Crown and the burghers in the towns who attempted to assert their autonomy from monarchical control. It is for this reason that Anthony Giddens (1984) has suggested that we should refer to social systems like this, not as 'class societies', but as 'class-divided societies', for while they exhibited class inequalities, they were not primarily organised around the relations between the classes.

Class may not be the most basic social division

A second problem with the Marxist approach is that, even in modern-day capitalist countries, class may not be the basic source of division, conflict, interest and identity. The division between men and women, for example, is in some respects more pertinent in affecting people's social relations and life chances than that between owners and non-owners of capital. A glance at the social composition of various key bodies – Parliament, the Stock Exchange, the General Committee of the TUC, the Church of England Synod, the Senate of Oxford or Cambridge Universities, the boardrooms of major companies – swiftly reveals that, although there is often a skewed recruitment in terms of class, there is generally an even more marked maldistribution of members in terms of gender. Similarly, women are frequently paid less than men for doing equivalent kinds of job, they may be discriminated against when it comes to recruitment or promotion, and they are still overwhelmingly responsible in most domestic households for carrying out the bulk of the housework. Little wonder, then, that some feminists have argued that gender relations, grounded in an enduring system of 'patriarchy', are far more significant than class divisions in shaping life chances and the organisation of power in modern societies.

There are other factors too which Marxist theory seems ill-equipped to recognise as basic to contemporary systems of social stratification. One obvious one is race and ethnicity. In countries like South Africa and Israel, racial and ethnic identity is absolutely fundamental in structuring people's access to social resources, but this is also true in other countries as well. In the Soviet Union, there is clear evidence of discrimination in jobs and other areas such as housing against certain ethnic groups like Jews and Latvians. In the United States, and particularly in the Deep South, it is still a major disadvantage to be black or Hispanic, while in Australia, the Aborigines remain largely excluded from the mainstream economic, political and cultural life of the country. In Britain too, of course, statistics on housing, employment, education and so on all reveal a clear pattern of disadvantage in respect of 'ethnic minorities', although it is important to distinguish here between the Afro-Caribbean community, which seems particularly disadvantaged on many of these dimensions, and those from the Indian sub-continent

13

who have often been more successful in overcoming the discrimination and prejudice directed against them.

Nor are gender and ethnicity the only 'missing variables' in Marxist approaches to social stratification. Religious persuasion can be a crucial factor – for example, in places like Northern Ireland and the Middle East. So too can national identity: for many millions of Basques, Bretons, Scots, Ukrainians, Moldavians, Lithuanians, Quebeckers, Tibetans, Mongolians and Palestinians, the basic issue which shapes their lives concerns not their class membership but their desire to live under the laws of a nation-state other than that to which they are subject. The sociological analysis of stratification has too often forgotten that divisions between classes can pale into insignificance for people who feel that they belong to an ethno-cultural grouping which is alien to the nation-state in which they live.

Marxism has at various times attempted to integrate such factors into its class analysis. Socialist feminists have sometimes argued, for example, that the patterns of domination inscribed in patriarchy are sustained by the system of class domination deriving from capitalism, although such arguments are rarely convincing, given that gender divisions predate capitalist class divisions by several thousand years. Similarly, there is a long history in Marxist thought which explains racist exclusion as a product of capitalism and the imperialist impulse in capitalist states. Again, though, the analysis lacks plausibility, for discrimination and domination on the basis of ethnicity was around long before modern capitalism. There is, furthermore, a sense in which free market capitalism, rather than generating racism, can be said to help undermine it. A rational capitalist entrepreneur will be interested in recruiting suitable labour at the lowest cost, no matter what colour the skin of those workers may be, just as a rational consumer will seek out the best buys without regard to the colour of the people who produced the goods in question. In South Africa today, the whites who are pushing most strongly for the dismantling of Apartheid are often those who are involved in running major capitalist enterprises, for a system which allocates people to jobs and areas by their colour rather than by their aptitudes is profoundly anti-capitalist in its logic.

The rise of the middle class and the fragmentary class structure

A third major problem with the Marxist approach concerns its commitment to a dual class model. If class is defined in terms of ownership or non-ownership of the means of production, then it is difficult to see how a 'middle class' can arise. Marx and his followers have recognised that the two main classes in capitalist societies are often fragmented into what they call 'class fractions'. The bourgeoisie, for example, consists of industrialists, financiers, merchants and land-owners, and these different fractions often find themselves in conflict. Industrialists may resent paying increased rents to landowners, or merchants may complain bitterly at the interest charged on the money they borrow from banks. Similarly, the proletariat is also divided between people in secure employment and those (the 'lumpenproletariat') who drift in and out of employment, and between direct producers of goods and those employed in service industries such as retailing or the financial sector. Further, Marx also recognises that not everybody in capitalist societies necessarily belongs to one of the two great classes since certain strata, such as the peasantry in France or the aristocracy in England, may still be in evidence from earlier historical periods. Nevertheless, neither the theory of class fractions, nor the recognition of class residues, can help to explain how it is that in most advanced capitalist countries, a distinct 'middle class' has grown up over the last hundred years. Marxist theory confronts a real and unresolved problem in dealing with groups like managers, civil servants, doctors, computer programmers and the millions of others who draw a salary yet in most other respects seem most unlike proletarians.

15

Groups like these rarely own much, if any, productive capital, yet some of them employ people, they often issue commands to other workers and make decisions about how capitalist enterprises should be run, and they are usually well-remunerated and quite highly esteemed. Defining them as 'working-class' seems no more plausible than defining them as capitalists.

Marxism has often skirted around this problem by referring to 'the bourgeoisie' as an ill-defined, catch-all category embracing both capitalists and middle classes, but this simply ducks the issue. Over the last ten years or so, various Marxist theorists have attempted to theorise such groups as a distinct 'middle class' or 'new petty bourgeoisie', but this work has rarely been convincing, and has normally entailed a significant break with the idea that classes arise around the ownership and non-ownership of the means of production.

For example, the Greek Marxist, Nicos Poulantzas, tried to theorise what he termed the 'new petty bourgeoisie' by suggesting that any employee who was engaged in mental labour, or who had responsibility for supervising other workers, or who was not employed directly in production, should be deemed 'petty bourgeois', but the result made little sense. Included in Poulantzas's identification of the 'middle class' were not only managers and professionals, but also service workers such as garage forecourt attendants, supervisory workers such as foremen, and so on.

Other attempts at resolving the problem have been just as unsuccessful. The American Marxist, Erik Olin Wright, identified three main classes in capitalist societies – capitalists, who own the means of production, workers, and small, independent business people (for example, the self-employed) whom he termed the 'petty bourgeoisie'. He then went on to argue that many people fall between these three classes into what he termed 'contradictory class locations'. Managers and supervisors, for example, are involved in running capitalist enterprises, yet they are also employees of these enterprises, and in this sense they occupy a class location midway between capitalists and workers. Similarly, many technical and professional workers enjoy substantial job autonomy, as the petty bourgeoisie do, but are not self-employed, and they therefore find themselves in a position between the capitalist and petty bourgeois classes. According to Wright, people in these contradictory locations may be pulled to one or other class pole – their allegiance shifts and they are there to be won by either side.

Yet this sort of analysis does not really resolve the problem either, and Wright himself has recently confused matters even further by revising his schema and coming up with a new twelve-class model! What seems to be going on in work like this is little more than a redescription of the troublesome strata, but as the classificatory systems expand, so the power of Marx's original insights get watered down. The strength of Marx's own analysis was that it identified two classes locked into an antagonistic yet mutually dependent relationship – capital and labour could not live together and could not live apart. This was then used to explain what Marx saw as the inherent and perpetual class struggle in capitalist societies – a struggle which represented the motor of social change. In modern formulations, however, this dynamic, relational idea of class has been lost, and we end up with elaborate descriptions of different positions in society with little idea of how they relate to each other.

Marxism is ill-suited to analysing the growth and significance of the middle class simply because an analysis which theorises classes in terms of relations to the means of production is necessarily dichotomous. Either people own the means of production, or they do not. Attempts to build a middle class into this schema will inevitably end up fudging the theory. Furthermore, the whole thrust of Marxist theory has always been that 'intermediate classes' should be disappearing rather than increasing in size and importance. Marx himself developed the view that, as capitalism progresses, so the stark gap between the bourgeoisie and the working class grows ever wider. The theory predicted that class antagonisms

17

would become clearer as the gulf between the two main classes became deeper, and those in the middle would be squeezed out into one or other of the two hostile camps. Yet what has actually happened is that class lines have become blurred, the middle class has grown in size and the stark nineteenth-century split between the haves and the have-nots has been confused as living standards have risen all round. The clear division which existed in the nineteenth century between capitalists and workers has broken down, for most large companies are no longer owned by particular individuals or families, but by insurance companies, unit trust funds and pension funds, all of which invest the savings of millions of ordinary workers in capitalist enterprises. This failure of Marx's prediction of social polarisation has been a major blow for the theory as a whole, for in the last hundred years the working class has become smaller, better off and decidedly less revolutionary in its fervour.

Working-class consciousness and intellectual wishful thinking

Yet another problem for Marxist class analysis has concerned the question of class consciousness. As we saw earlier, Engels very early on introduced the idea of 'false consciousness' to account for the fact that many working-class people do not see their situation in the way that Marxist theory does, and this concept has since been pressed into service by many theorists to account for the lack of proletarian revolutionary zeal. Some, like the guru of the sixties' student movement, Herbert Marcuse, have argued that the workers have been bedazzled by consumerism. Thus Marcuse argued that capitalism has implanted 'false needs' into workers' consciousness in such a way that they have been fobbed off with cars and washing machines while all the time remaining in a state of alienation and exploitation. Others, like the French philosopher Louis Althusser, have blamed 'ideological state apparatuses' such as the schools and the media for reproducing the illusory idea that we are individuals in control of our own destiny, thereby concealing the truth of class power. Still others, such as the influential German Marxist, Jurgen Habermas, have written of a 'systematically distorted communication' which prevents us from developing autonomous thought and an effective critique of the system in which we live.

All of these approaches suffer from the same two problems. First, they beg the question of how Marxist theorists can claim to know the truth when it is concealed from everybody else. Despite many elaborate and ingenious attempts at answering this question, we are always ultimately left with an unsubstantiated claim to privileged insight involving a wholly circular argument: Marxists know the true situation because Marxist theory is true! And secondly, all these variants on the theme of false consciousness end up haughtily dismissive of what working-class people themselves say and think about their situation. The abstract class is thought to be the repository of a true socialist consciousness while the flesh and blood individuals who make up that class are ignored. As Frank Parkin puts it, writers like Marcuse and Althusser seem to offer a 'diagnosis implying in the most oblique and scholarly manner that the proletariat was suffering from a kind of collective brain damage' (1979: 81).

These factors – the insensitivity to systems of stratification other than those based on class, the failure to theorise divisions grounded in gender and ethnicity, the inability to explain the growth of the middle class within capitalism, and the unwillingness to consider actual forms of class consciousness as opposed to idealised ones – all fundamentally undermine Marxist approaches to social stratification. These are not the only problems with this approach – the theory of exploitation, for example, can be challenged, as can the view that capital and labour represent inherently irreconcilable interests – but many sociologists have felt that they are enough to justify a search for an alternative approach.

19

The Weberian alternative

Max Weber was a German historian and sociologist writing mainly in the early years of this century. It has been suggested that Weber engaged in a 'dialogue with the ghost of Marx', for he addressed many of the issues at the heart of Marx's theory but came to very different conclusions.

Weber's sociology was based in a commitment to 'methodological individualism'. In other words, while Weber recognised that it is useful to employ collective concepts such as 'social class', he argued that these were simply shorthand labels for aggregates of individuals. Unlike Marx, who saw classes as real social entities, Weber used the term to refer simply to groups within a population who shared certain common economic characteristics.

Weber's principal concern in his work on stratification was with the exercise of power and the organisation of domination in human societies. He suggested that there were three kinds of situation in which one group of people might expect to get its own way in relationships with another group of people. First, power could arise on the basis of unequal access to material resources. If I have something that you want or need, then I am in a position to exercise power over you. Weber referred to this as *class power*. Second, power can be a function of social status and esteem. If you look up to me or believe that I am in some way your social superior, then again you are likely to defer to my wishes and commands. Weber saw this as *social power* – the power exercised by *status groups* as opposed to classes. Third, one group may dominate another through the agency of the state, either by directly controlling it, or by influencing those who do control it. As Weber emphasised, the state is the only institution in modern societies which claims the right to force people to do things. If I do not pay my taxes, or fail to send my children to school, or try to publish what the state deems to be secret, then I can be sent to jail. This state use of 'legitimate coercion' is referred to by Weber as *political power* exercised by *parties*, by which he meant not only formal political parties, but any organised interests which seek to influence the operations of the state.

This approach to power is different from that of Marx in four important ways. First, it distinguishes three dimensions of power in society which Marxist theory elides. For Weber, unlike Marx, the group which enjoys most class power is not necessarily the same as the group with social power or the group with political power. Put another way, wealth, status and influence are not necessarily synonymous. This insight enables us to recognise that some groups may be politically powerful without being particularly wealthy (trade union leaders might be one example), or that the most prestigious strata (for example, the old landed aristocracy with its titles and exclusive haunts) are not necessarily the most economically powerful interests in the land, or that those who own considerable wealth are not automatically to be thought of as a political 'ruling class'.

Weber's approach also allows us to analyse power and domination on the basis of gender and ethnicity, for it tells us that people in the same class situation (for example, black and white factory workers or male and female barristers) may nevertheless share very different status positions. Black workers, for example, may be looked down upon by their white colleagues and excluded from various privileges even though they do the same job for the same money. Similarly, the female barrister may find it difficult to secure cases because of suspicion or hostility on the part of male solicitors, and she may well find that her career is hindered by domestic responsibilities which her male colleagues are not called upon to perform. Thus, unlike the Marxist approach, Weberian stratification theory is *multi-dimensional*, and this enables it to analyse both class and non-class bases of inequality.

Second, this same division between economic, social and political power also means that Weber could analyse non-capitalist societies without falling into the ethnocentric error of assuming that they were all class societies. The Indian caste system, for example, is an almost pure example of a system of

21

stratification based on status, or 'social honour'. As we saw above, the distinctions between different castes are rigid yet have little to do with wealth as such. Rather, caste, like all forms of status, is defined in terms of lifestyles – the kinds of occupation you do, whom you marry, how and what you eat, and most crucially, your parentage. Weber recognised that, with the advent of modern capitalism, such status-based social orders tended to recede, and class systems of stratifi-cation became more important, but he also pointed out that status power has been far from eclipsed in modern societies.

Third, the way in which Weber defined class was very different from Marx's approach. In the Weberian tradition, class is a function of *market power* rather than ownership or non-ownership of the means of production. Seen in this way, people form a class if they share roughly common life chances. They may enjoy similar life chances because they own substantial property holdings from which they can earn a profit, but the property market is not the only factor which influences our economic situation. What is also crucial is our position in the labour market. Some people have particular skills or abilities which enable them to command high wages when they take their labour to the market, and this too will affect their class position. For Weber, then, class has to do with both property and occupation. In his terms, there are positively and negatively privileged *property classes*, but there are also positively and negatively privileged occupational or *commercial classes*.

It is not therefore the case that if people do not own property such as land, banks or factories, they are all proletarian, for some will be more powerful in the labour market than others and will therefore be able to secure greater material rewards. It is this which allows Weber to identify the nature of the middle class under capitalism in a way that Marx could not. For Weber, the upper class consists of those who live off property income and enjoy the privileges of edu-cation. The lower class, by contrast, is 'negatively privileged' on both dimensions. They neither own resources which can be

22

used to generate revenue, nor do they have the education which could bring them a high salary. In between these two classes, the middle class consists of people who have some property but little education (the 'petty bourgeoisie' such as small shopkeepers and entrepreneurs), and people who have little property but can command high wages by virtue of their education and qualifications (the 'intelligentsia and specialists'). This latter group, of course, is precisely the stratum which has been growing fastest over the last hundred years.

Fourth, Weber was alert to the subjective aspect of stratification. The various classes which he identified do not exist as real entities unless and until their members come to think of themselves in class terms. Marx too understood this, but for him, it was axiomatic that the working class would gradually develop a class consciousness which would lead to a revolutionary insurrection against the bourgeoisie. For Weber, whether or not people come to think and act in class terms is an open question. In some situations, and for some purposes, they may do, but they may equally organise themselves around other interests and identities. Political conflicts could take the form of class struggles (for example, strikes by unions or demonstrations by left-wing parties), but they may also involve the mobilisation of status groups (as in black movements or feminist politics, for example), and they are sometimes based in neither class nor status affiliations (pro- and anti-abortion campaigns, the 'peace movement', and so on). In Weber's sociology there is no space for a concept like 'false consciousness', for people act in ways that are meaning-ful to them given the values that they hold, and it makes no sense for a sociological observer to criticise these values as 'false', nor to dismiss people's actions as in some ethical way 'wrong' or 'misguided'.

The legacy of Marx and Weber

Contemporary sociological work on class and stratification has been strongly influenced by the writings of both Marx and

Weber. Today work continues in both traditions. Judgement as to their relative worth is almost inevitably clouded by personal and political values.

The main reason for this is simply that Marx was never just a social scientist; he was a political revolutionary. One of his most famous comments, which is engraved on his tomb in Highgate cemetery in London, was that, 'The philosophers have only interpreted the world in various ways; the point, however, is to change it.' Marxist theory is thus inextricably bound up with the political project of revolution. Those who seek to challenge capitalism are generally attracted to this theory with its view of modern society as two warring camps and its vision of a future socialist world. Many left-wing sociologists therefore endorse the basic outlines of Marx's approach while at the same time recognising that the theory has to be revised to take account of the changed conditions of the late twentieth century. The problem with contemporary Marxism, however, is that nobody has yet been able to find a way of revising the theory while remaining faithful to the basic ideas set down by its founder.

The principal alternative to Marxist theory in the field of social stratification is that established by Weber. This approach is not without its problems either: Marxist critics claim, for example, that Weberian approaches fail to under-stand the structural basis of class antagonisms and over-emphasise the division between economic and political power in advanced capitalism.

Theorists within each of these traditions could (and possibly will) continue their argument for years without reaching any point of agreement or compromise. Perhaps, therefore, we should evaluate these two perspectives in terms of their empirical validity rather than their theoretical assumptions. As we shall see in the next chapter, a study by Gordon Marshall and his colleagues at the University of Essex has recently done precisely this, and their results suggest that it is probably more useful to analyse contemporary class relations using a Weberian model than it is employing

Marxist concepts. Their findings are not conclusive – such findings rarely are – but taken together with the serious theoretical problems which remain unresolved in contemporary Marxist theory, they do suggest that a Weberian emphasis on differences in market power is likely to prove more useful in understanding the British class system than a Marxist focus on ownership of the means of production.

Activity

Marx and Weber differ in the way they approach each of the following questions. For each question, write one paragraph outlining *how* they differ.

How is social class to be defined?
How is someone's class membership determined?
What is the relation between economic wealth and political power?
How universal are class systems in human history?
Do classes exist if people do not recognise them?

Further reading

The single best secondary source on the issues discussed in this chapter is Anthony Giddens (1973) The Class Structure of the Advanced Societies, *London: Hutchinson – see especially the first five chapters. Important and pertinent critiques of Marxist class theory can be found in Frank Parkin (1979)* Marxism and Class Theory: A Bourgeois Critique, *London: Tavistock, and David Lockwood, 'The weakest link in the chain?', in David Rose (ed.) (1988)* Social Stratification and Economic Change, *London: Hutchinson. A rather easier source is Tom Bottomore (1965)* Classes in Modern Society, *London: Allen & Unwin, ch. 2.*

Some of the key primary sources are quite readable and accessible. For Marx, start with Part One of The Manifesto of the Communist Party. *This can be followed by the essays on 'The Eighteenth Brumaire of Louis Bonaparte' (sections 1, 2, 3 and 7) and 'Civil War in France' (Engels's introduction and Part Three). All three essays can be found in the single volume of Marx and Engels (1968) Selected Works, London: Lawrence and Wishart. For Weber, see his* Economy and Society *(1968), New York: Bedminster Press, Part One: ch. 4 and Part Two: pp. 926–39. The first of these essays can also be found in Max Weber (1947)* The Theory of Social and Economic Organisation, *New York: Oxford University Press, pp. 424–9, and the second is reprinted in H. Gerth and C. Wright Mills (eds) (1948)* From Max Weber, *London: Routledge & Kegan Paul. Also useful is Peter Worsley (1982)* Marx and Marxism, *London: Tavistock.*

2

Social class and social inequality in Britain

From theory to systems of classification

Sociologists down the years have devoted much time and thought to the theoretical problems raised in class analysis, yet empirical studies have often persisted in classifying people in very crude and atheoretical ways.

The manual / non-manual division

One example of this is the use of simple manual/non-manual class distinctions. Some of the classic post-war sociological studies grounded their analyses in this division – Young and Wilmott (1957) *Family and Kinship in East London* drew a fundamental dichotomy between professional and clerical workers on the one hand and manual workers on the other (see, for example, p. 171), and Douglas's study of the effects of social class on educational attainment similarly distinguished the middle class from the working class according

27

to whether children's fathers were in non-manual or manual occupations (Douglas *et al.* 1968).

There are two major problems with this sort of approach. The first is that there is little or no basis in social theory for dividing the population according to whether or not people work with their hands. This means that our theoretical categories such as 'working class' or 'middle class' do not correspond to the empirical categories through which data are gathered. Such studies can therefore tell us little about patterns of class inequality since the strata they identify are not classes as such.

The second problem is that the manual/non-manual division swiftly becomes confusing if not downright misleading. On what basis, for example, is a routine clerical worker held to be in a higher class than a skilled lathe-turner? The latter may well be better off financially, more highly skilled and may lead a very similar way of life. Furthermore, many so-called 'white-collar' jobs are today filled by women and they often have lower wages, lower status and less job autonomy than many predominantly male manual occupations. To designate such women as members of a higher class-grouping simply because they do not get their hands dirty seems curious, to say the least.

Some researchers, recognising the limited validity of simple manual/non-manual dichotomies, have instead made use of the advertising industry's system of classification by which people are allocated to classes A, B, C and so on according to patterns of spending and consumption which are associated with different occupational groupings. Such an approach may well prove fruitful for firms seeking to find out about their potential customers for a given product, but for sociological purposes they are little better than the dichotomous models. Such schema bear no relation to the class theories developed within either Marxist or Weberian approaches and their usefulness in sociological analysis is therefore extremely limited.

A rather more discriminatory system of classification which is often employed in empirical social research is that used by the government's own Office of Population Censuses and Surveys. Since 1911, the OPCS has listed thousands of occupational titles and has then classified them into a much smaller number of ranked social groupings. The system of classification has changed over the years, but the most recent, devised for the 1981 census, allocates people to one of six classes on the basis of their occupation and their 'employment status' (such as manager, foreman or whatever). The first two of these classes include managers, administrators and professionals. The third basically includes white-collar occupations with limited or no authority, and the final three refer respectively to skilled, semi-skilled and unskilled manual workers.

While this system can be useful, and is certainly preferable to simple manual/non-manual distinctions or to the A to E gradings used in market research, the theoretical rationale behind it is still far from clear. In 1971, the OPCS claimed that it was an attempt to group classes according to their 'standing in the community' (what Weber would have recognised as a status criterion). In 1981, essentially the same six groupings were said to reflect 'levels of occupational skill' (or what Weber would have recognised as a differentiation of commercial classes). Sociologists have often criticised such ambiguity in what the OPCS schema is actually meant to refer to, and at the time of writing it is again under review. By the time of the 1991 census it seems likely that a new nine-fold 'Standard Occupational Classification' system will be in operation which will classify groups by their level and area of competence, and this may come to replace the existing six-class model.

A problem common to both of these models is that, by relying on occupational data for sorting people into classes, the majority of the population who are not in paid work get left out. There are two points here. One is that these schemes ignore the class of wealthy people who live solely from income from property – in a sense, they are blind to the existence of the 'upper class'. The other is that they also have difficulty classifying people like housewives, the unemployed, pensioners and students to any given class. The census itself tries to resolve this problem by classifying people according to the social class of the 'head of household', but this is far from satisfactory.

What is clearly needed is a system of classification which can be employed fairly easily in empirical work but which is also grounded in a coherent theory of social stratification, be it Marxist, Weberian or any other. And in recent years, sociologists have begun to develop just such an approach.

Activity

For this exercise you will need a copy of the OPCS *Classification of Occupations 1980* (HMSO 1980). Find which of the Registrar-General's social classes the following people belong to:

A primary school teacher

A self-employed jewellery designer who does not employ any helpers

A bus driver

The manager of a small mini-cab firm

A detective inspector in the police force

Note: To classify an occupation, first look up the job title in the index of occupations between pp. 6–109. Write down the code number which you find there, and look this up in Appendix G (pp. 111–14). This will give you a code reflecting both occupation and employment status. You then use this code to look up the class of the person in Appendix B1 (pp. lxxxiv–civ).

If several people do this exercise independently, you should then check all the results against each other. How many discrepancies are there? How reliable and foolproof is this system of classification?

David Lockwood's development of Weber's class analysis

The origins of this work lie in David Lockwood's study of the class situation of clerks, published in 1958 as *The Blackcoated Worker*. Developing Weber's distinction between classes and status groups, Lockwood argued that the position of clerks had to be considered in terms of three aspects – their market situation, work situation and status situation.

The market situation refers to the income which clerks can attain in the labour market, the security of their employment, the fringe benefits available to them, and so on. The work situation refers to the extent to which clerks can exercise autonomy and discretion in their work, the sort of surveillance to which they are subject, whether or not they come into contact with their boss, and the skills they need to exercise in their day-to-day life in the office. Finally, the status situation refers to the esteem in which clerks are held in our society and their ability to sustain prestige in the face of changes such as the feminisation and the mechanisation of the office.

Lockwood's conclusion was that, although the status of clerks was changing, their work and market situations were still sufficiently distinctive to explain their view of themselves as a class set apart from manual workers. Put another way, the study disputed the claim that groups like clerks were being 'proletarianised' as a result of deskilling, declining incomes and erosion of status.

Lockwood's distinction between work, market and status situations has since been used in a variety of studies including his own later research with Goldthorpe, Bechhofer and Platt (1969) which refuted the claim that well-paid manual workers were becoming middle-class (a claim which was found to be just as invalid as the idea that clerks were becoming working-class). We consider this particular study in more detail later in Chapter five. For now, the important point to note about Lockwood's work is not the findings but the approach, for his identification of the three key dimensions of stratification has proved theoretically useful as well as empirically fruitful.

John Goldthorpe's neo-Weberian class model

A good example of the way in which this approach has been developed is the elaborate class schema devised by John Goldthorpe over the course of his work on social mobility in Britain. Goldthorpe uses information on occupation and employment status just as the OPCS does, but he then allocates people to social classes on the explicit criteria of their work and market situations. The idea, in other words, is to identify clusters of people who typically share similar amounts of authority and autonomy in the workplace (the work situation) and who at the same time also share roughly common life chances and economic interests by virtue of their situation in the labour market. Like the OPCS schema, this approach still fails to consider classes distinguished by property as opposed to occupation, and it also shares similar problems as regards its usefulness in analysing the class position of women whose occupational profile is very different from that of men (a point which has led some critics to suggest that an entirely different class schema is required for each gender). Nevertheless, the final result is more systematic and theoretically meaningful than that achieved by using the OPCS scale, for the different class categories refer not to vague and unsubstantiated notions about 'standing in the community' and the like, but to clear differences in people's economic power in society.

Goldthorpe's schema has several versions. At its fullest it identifies eleven social classes, but such a refined system of differentiation is difficult to use in most empirical studies where researchers are interested in correlating class position with other variables such as educational success, housing conditions, mortality rates, or whatever. The eleven classes, therefore, have often been collapsed, sometimes into seven, but most commonly into five main classes. These are: the *service class*, also referred to as the *salariat*, consisting of professional and administrative employees, managers, proprietors and higher technicians and supervisors; *routine non-manual workers*, a category which includes personal service workers such as shop assistants and secretaries; the *petty bourgeoisie*, made up of small proprietors, self-employed manual workers and farmers; *lower technicians and supervisors*, including foremen; and the *working class* which includes skilled as well as semi- and unskilled manual workers, and also embraces agricultural workers.

This five-class model is sometimes then further collapsed by combining the three intermediate classes into one, leaving a conception of the key divisions in the British class structure as those between the salariat, the intermediate classes, and the working class. It is this model, for example, which was used in the analysis of voting patterns in the 1983 general election (see Heath, Jowell and Curtice 1985).

For all its faults, Goldthorpe's is arguably the most helpful class model we have available in contemporary British sociology. This has been painstakingly demonstrated by Marshall, Newby, Rose and Vogler (1988) who set out to evaluate the OPCS model, Erik Olin Wright's revised Marxist model, and Goldthorpe's neo-Weberian model. They conducted a survey of 2,000 people in Britain and then coded each of their respondents according to all three class models. They found that the Goldthorpe schema was most successful in avoiding anomalies and discrepancies (Wright's approach, for example, led to some lawyers and some cleaners being included in the same class category as 'semi-autonomous employees'), that it was best suited to analysing new and important class positions, and that it corresponded most closely to how interviewees themselves thought about their class situation.

Of course, the Goldthorpe model is not without its problems. The more the eleven classes are collapsed, into seven, five or even three, in order to ease empirical analysis, the blunter and less sensitive the analysis becomes. There are also problems about how women are to be analysed in this model, for Marshall and his colleagues are critical of Goldthorpe's belief that whole families can be classified according to the social class of the male 'head of household'. And another major problem with Goldthorpe's approach is its exclusive focus on what Weber would term commercial classes and its neglect of property classes, for this is another example of an occupation-based system of classification which neglects ownership of property. This weakness may be very significant when we remember that property ownership today is not as concentrated in a few hands as it used to be. As we shall now see, the economic situation of millions of people in Britain is affected, not only by the work they do, but by the property holdings (in the form of housing, pension rights, shares and so on) to which they have title. At some point in the future, sociologists will have to take this into account in devising class models, but as yet this has not seriously been attempted, and the Goldthorpe scale seems to be the most acceptable option currently on offer.

Class, wealth and income

Analysis of income and wealth statistics is fraught with hazards. The data themselves can be extremely unreliable, and the interpretation of the data (including judgements of what kind of evidence is relevant or irrelevant) can easily lend itself to supporting whichever political argument the researcher seeks to 'prove'.

The distribution of wealth

For example, it can be shown through an analysis of estate duties that the proportion of the nation's wealth owned by the richest 1 per cent of the population has fallen quite dramatically through the twentieth century. Does this there- fore justify the claim that the distribution of wealth has become less unequal? In one sense, of course, it does, yet

Atkinson (1972) was able to show that while the richest 1 per cent had been losing wealth, the next 4 per cent had been gaining it! His explanation was that the introduction of death duties before the First World War had led families to spread their holdings among more family members in order to reduce their tax liability. This hardly amounts to a dramatic shift in the pattern of wealth-holding in the country as a whole.

Or to take a contrary example, if we compare the percentage of the nation's wealth owned personally by, say, the poorest 10 per cent of the population, we can show that there has been little change since the turn of the century. The poor did not own much, if anything, in 1900, and they do not own much more now. But to conclude from this that there has been no redistribution of wealth would be highly misleading, for groups slightly higher up the scale have undoubtedly improved their relative wealth over this period. In 1914, for example, only one household in ten in England and Wales owned the home it lived in, yet by 1986, this figure had risen to 65 per cent (*Housing and Construction Statistics*, 1987). If housing is included in calculations of personal wealth-holdings, there is no doubt that there has been a major shift in the way ownership of the nation's assets is distributed.

Where there is general agreement is on the fact that the distribution of wealth in Britain is more uneven than the distribution of incomes. According to Lord Diamond's Royal Commission on the Distribution of Income and Wealth, the richest 1 per cent of the population in 1972 owned 28 per cent of the total wealth, much of it in the form of land. The Commission suggested that this represented a fall from a 69 per cent share in 1911. Taken together, the top 5 per cent owned 54 per cent of wealth, the top 10 per cent owned 67 per cent, and the top 20 per cent owned 82 per cent, leaving just 18 per cent of the nation's assets in the hands of four-fifths of the population.

This remarkably skewed distribution appears less unequal when assets like pension rights are included in the calculations. The logic behind this is that pension rights represent a claim on revenues from assets such as land and stocks and shares which pension funds invest in on behalf of their members. Adjusting for this, the Commission found that the proportion of total wealth owned by the richest 1 per cent fell from 28 per cent to 13 per cent. Similarly, estimates by Halsey (in *Social Trends*, 1987) suggest that in 1985, the richest 1 per cent of the population in Britain owned 21 per cent of the marketable wealth (that is, assets which could be sold), but that this figure fell to 12 per cent when non-marketable assets such as pension rights were included.

Recent trends in the distribution of wealth in Britain

Any discussion of the distribution of wealth in Britain should pay particular attention to the sociological significance of three recent trends. One, already referred to, is the spread of home-ownership. Owner-occupation is no longer the prerogative of the well-to-do – in 1985, 66 per cent of skilled manual and own-account workers owned their homes, as did 44 per cent of semi-skilled and personal service workers and 33 per cent of unskilled manual workers (*General Household Survey*, 1987). Since 1980, working-class home-ownership in particular has shown a marked increase following the Conservative government's 'Right to buy' legislation which has enabled nearly one million former council tenants to purchase their homes from their local authority landlords, often at substantial discounts. The result has been a major redistribution of wealth from the state to private households. Of course, owner-occupied housing varies enormously in its value, both between different kinds of houses, and between different regions of the country. Nevertheless, for the first time in British history, nearly two-thirds of the population now owns an asset of considerable value – an asset, furthermore, which tends to increase in value with inflation and which can be handed on to the next generation. It is true to say that most sociologists have not yet come to terms with the potential significance for British society of such a large proportion of the population being in a position for the first time to accumulate wealth in the form of physical property and to pass it on through inheritance.

The other two themes concern the spread of private pensions, which now cover half or more of all workers, and the growth of personal shareholdings, either directly or through unit trusts and Personal Equity Plans. As with housing, so too with shareholdings: a dramatic redistribution of wealth from the state to private individuals has taken place since 1980, partly due to the Conservative government's policy of privatising state sector utilities such as Gas and Telecommunications and industrial firms like Jaguar and BP. In 1979, less than 5 per cent of Britons owned any shares; by 1987, a survey conducted for OPCS found that at least 19 per cent did so. Most of these, of course, own very small holdings of shares – more than half of all personal shareholders own shares worth £1,000 or less – and shareholding declines as one moves from the salariat, through the intermediate classes, to the working class. Nevertheless, the spread of home-ownership, pension rights and direct and indirect shareholding is certainly transforming the picture of wealth distribution by creating a large 'middle stratum' of small property owners in between the few who own a lot and the residualised minority who own virtually nothing. This is a point to which we shall return later.

Income distribution

Despite these recent developments, the overall pattern of wealth-holding still appears highly unequal. Incomes too are unequally distributed, but the contrasts are nowhere near as great. According to the Royal Commission, for example, the top 1 per cent of income earners took 5 per cent of total incomes in 1972/3, while the bottom 80 per cent earned over 60 per cent of total income.

As with wealth, so with incomes; we have to be cautious in assembling and interpreting our data. In *Social Trends*, the

37

annual digest of official statistics on various aspects of social life in Britain, income figures are broken down into three categories: *original income*, which refers to total income before taxes and benefits are taken into account; *disposable income*, which is the total amount of money people receive from all sources less the taxes and other deductions they have to pay; and *final income*, which is calculated to include the imputed value of those services and goods such as health care and schooling which the state provides and which people consume without extra payment.

Looking at the distribution of original incomes in 1984, the top 20 per cent earned 49 per cent of total incomes while the bottom 20 per cent earned just 0.3 per cent. These figures look dramatic but are not surprising, for many people have no income other than what they receive in benefits and allowances. When these are taken into account, as of course they must be, the share of disposable income accruing to the top 20 per cent drops slightly to 40 per cent, while that of the bottom 20 per cent increases twenty-two times to nearly 7 per cent. One might imagine that the figures on final income would reveal a further shift towards a narrowing of differentials, but this is not in fact the case. Thus, figures for final income (which includes the value of 'free' services consumed) show the top 20 per cent holding 39 per cent, while the bottom 20 per cent gets just over 7 per cent.

The reason why figures for disposable income and final income hardly vary is quite simply that high income earners often benefit just as much if not more from state welfare services than do the poorest sections of the population. Around 95 per cent of the population with school age children, for example, takes advantage of the 'free' state education system, and 90 per cent of the population relies entirely on the National Health Service for its medical needs. This means that high income earners receive an indirect boost to their income just as much as those who get by on basic state benefits. Indeed, the value of the welfare state for higher earners is often greater than for those on low incomes, for their children often stay longer in the state education system, they often make greater use of state medical facilities, and so on. In the absence of means-testing, universal services can often be regressive in their income effects (a phenomenon known in economics as 'Director's Law').

One final note of caution! All these figures on income and wealth refer to individuals. This can itself be misleading, however, for most people live in households with at least one other person (single-person households have been growing but still only account for 24 per cent of the total). In many of these cases, the household budget will reflect receipt of two or more incomes, and the standard of living available to a dual income household can often far exceed that of a household with only one earner, even if he or she receives a relatively high wage. It could be argued, therefore, that the divisions between multi-earner, single-earner and no-earner households are at least as significant as those between top, middle and bottom income bands. Given that none of the statistics which we have been considering look at households, as opposed to individuals, the picture of income distribution which emerges from them is at the very least incomplete.

It is clear from all this evidence that Britain is an unequal society. Ownership of wealth is highly skewed, although recent developments have increased the holdings of many people. Incomes are less unevenly distributed, but the gap between top and bottom is still considerable.

Such facts have still to be interpreted, however. Why do such inequalities persist? Are they necessarily 'unfair' or 'unjust'? Would it be possible to develop a different kind of society where resources were more evenly spread out? These are the issues to be addressed in the next chapter.

Further reading

For an excellent review of issues posed in the classification of social classes, see Catherine Marsh, 'Social class and occupation', in R. Burgess (ed.) (1986) Key Variables in

Social Investigation, *London: Routledge and Kegan Paul. The Goldthorpe schema can be found in his* Social Mobility and Class Structure in Modern Britain *(1980), Oxford: Clarendon Press, ch. 2, and a full outline and evaluation is provided by Gordon Marshall* et al. *(1988)* Social Class in Modern Britain, *London: Hutchinson, chs. 2, 3, and 4. A useful accessible and up-to-date source on various indicators of income and wealth is the annual HMSO publication,* Social Trends.

3

Thinking about
social inequality

Unequal life chances

We saw in Chapter two that there is considerable inequality
of wealth in Britain, and that income distribution too is
uneven. These economic inequalities mean that different
sections of the population enjoy different life chances.
Obviously, different groups can afford different amounts and
qualities of the goods and services which are available in the
market. People with more money can afford better housing,
they can choose to run a car rather than rely on public
transport, they can take themselves off on more exotic
holidays, and so on. But economic inequalities do not end
there, for it is also often the case that higher social class
groups enjoy other advantages even when these do not
depend on the direct purchase of goods and services.

No matter how we define social class, statistics reveal that
lower-class groups do not live for as long (even though they
are entitled to free and universal health care), their children

are less well educated (even though they are entitled to the same quality of state education), and so on. Nor is class the only dimension on which such variations may occur. There are also well-documented inequalities between racial and ethnic groups – Afro-Caribbean children, for example, perform much worse in the education system than white children from the same sort of class background. Similarly, there is evidence that girls underachieve in secondary and further education as compared with boys of the same measured ability, that people living in different kinds of areas in different regions of the country have different levels of health and morbidity, and so on.

The existence of inequalities in Britain should come as no surprise, for ever since human beings first began planting crops and domesticating animals, human societies have generated inequalities between people. Indeed, compared with many societies of the past and of the present, Britain probably rates as one of the less unequal social orders which the world has witnessed. There is nothing remarkable about social inequality – given the history of humanity, what would be remarkable would be the discovery of a truly egalitarian society.

Later in this chapter we shall consider whether the universality of social inequality suggests that it is inherent or even necessary to any form of society. Before that, however, we shall ask whether inequalities such as those found in modern Britain can be justified. This is more a moral than a sociological question, but moral and political philosophers who have addressed it have developed arguments about 'social justice' which are directly relevant to sociological concerns in that they focus on the kinds of social arrangements within which inequalities may or may not be considered justifiable. We shall look at three different kinds of argument corresponding broadly to Marxist, social–democratic and liberal political philosophies.

What do we mean by 'equality'?

Before we start, it is as well to clarify what is meant by 'equality'. The term has at least three meanings. First, there is *legal* or formal equality – the idea that everybody is equal before the law and that everybody is subject to the same rules, and will be punished in the same way if they break them, irrespective of birth or social position. This is a relatively recent idea in human history, and many modern states still do not subscribe to it (South Africa is probably the best example). In Europe, the principle of legal equality developed during the seventeenth and eighteenth centuries at a time when the different estates had different legal rights and obligations. It reached its climax in the French Revolution of 1789 which rallied opposition to the *ancien régime* around the demand for (legal) equality, as well as liberty and fraternity. Today, most Western capitalist states, including Britain, are committed to upholding this notion of equality, although in practice it is not always applied as rigorously as it might be.

A second way in which equality is used is to refer to *equality of opportunity*. The idea here is that everybody should have an equal chance to achieve whatever they can through their merits (for this reason, a social organisation based on this principle is often referred to as a *meritocracy*). We shall consider how British society compares with this ideal when we look at evidence on social mobility. For now, we may note that it is often more difficult than it seems to ensure that everybody has an equal opportunity, for from the day that we are born, our chances in life diverge according to the sorts of parents we have, the availability of resources around us, the kinds of area we live in, and so on. Even if all parents were equally wealthy, there would still be marked inequalities of opportunity, for some parents would presumably give more time and affection to their children than others, as well as passing on different genetic advantages in terms of intelligence, strength, beauty or whatever.

The third conception of equality is *equality of outcome*. In this view, meritocracy is not enough. True equality means that everybody has the same, irrespective of their talents, efforts and abilities. If a meritocracy is like a race where everybody lines up together at the start, a fully-fledged egalitarian society would be like a perfectly handicapped race where everybody passes the finishing tape at the same time no matter how hard and fast they have tried to run.

Now it is crucial to understand that these three conceptions of equality are not consistent with one another. In particular, as Hayek (1960) has argued, the very attempt to bring about equality of opportunity or equality of outcome must undermine legal equality. This is because, in pursuing egalitarian ends, it is necessary to treat people differently rather than apply the same rules to everybody. Various 'affirmative action' and 'equal opportunity' programmes in Britain, the USA and elsewhere clearly reveal the nature of this problem. Where it is decided, for example, that blacks are disadvantaged in relation to whites, or women in relation to men, it then follows that equality of opportunity can only be achieved by discriminating *against* whites and males and *in favour of* blacks and females. The result is that different rules and criteria are applied to members of each group – for example, a woman may be appointed to a job, not because she is better qualified than a male competitor, but simply because she is female. This breaks the principle of equal treatment according to common rules and although it is motivated by different intentions, it is *in principle* no different from, say, the decision in South Africa to reserve different jobs for different racial groups. Similarly, the view that workers are disadvantaged in relation to employers underpins trade union laws which explicitly allow union members to do things which other individuals would be prevented from doing (such as restraint of trade by means of picketing and blacking). Again, the attempt to 'even up' a perceived imbalance has resulted in transgression of the principle of legal equality or 'blind justice'.

44

Marxist theory and social inequality

This clash beween the different conceptions of equality is not generally a problem for Marxist theory, for it dismisses the principle of legal equality as a convenient fiction of bourgeois ideology. The argument here is that there cannot ever be true legal equality between individuals in a society organised around the systematic inequality of classes. Marxists accept that different classes are subject to the same law in capitalist societies, so that rich capitalists who steal are in principle treated in the same way as any other thief. The point, however, is that the wealth of the capitalist has itself been achieved at the expense of other people since the relation between capital and labour is one of exploitation. The situation is akin to that of the stork and the fox in the fable by Aesop; the portions of food were served equally, but under conditions where only one was in a position to eat it.

It is for this reason that Marx was consistently dismissive of demands for equality. There could be no equality and no meaningful sense of fairness in a society organised as a system of exploitation. Marx always insisted that his critique of capitalism was not a moral critique. He did not oppose capitalism on the grounds that it was an unfair or unequal system, for he believed it was a mistake to focus on questions of distribution. His critique was, he believed, grounded in science, not ethics. It was because capitalism was exploitative that it was doomed to extinction, for such a system could not indefinitely hold down a working class whose lot could only worsen for as long as the system kept going. Marx looked forward to a future revolution in the same way that astronomers look forward to the next appearance of a comet or an eclipse of the moon: the revolution, like a comet, is neither morally good nor bad but historically inevitable.

Even when a new socialist society comes to be born, however, it seems clear that Marx shied away from support for equality of outcomes. The principle of distribution under socialism, he wrote, will be that of reward according to work

45

done, and everyone would have the same opportunity to contribute to the common good. As he explained,

> The individual producer receives back from society – after the deductions have been made – exactly what he gives to it. . . . He receives a certificate from society that he has furnished such and such an amount of labour (after deducting his labour for the common funds), and with this certificate he draws from the social stock of means of consumption as much as costs the same amount of labour.
>
> (Marx 1970: 319)

The well-known formula of 'From each according to his ability, to each according to his needs' could only be applicable in the conditions of a mature communist society which would follow socialism a long time later. Marx, in other words, was arguing not for equality of outcomes, but for equality of opportunity in the sense that everybody would be a worker and would receive whatever was the value of their efforts.

As things have turned out, however, even this diluted form of egalitarianism has proved impossible to implement. Following the 1917 uprising, Soviet economists spent many fruitless years trying to devise a means for calculating the value of different people's labour by applying Marx's theoretical writings. They failed because in practice it seems to be impossible to weigh up different skills, responsibilities, hardships and so on and to come to a rational judgement regarding the proportion of one person's labour which is equivalent to that of another's. As 'bourgeois' economists have been arguing for a long time, the value of someone's labour cannot be judged by what they do, but has to be assessed by what other people are prepared to pay for it. Seen in this way, the value to society of a teacher's work, or an acrobat's work, or a clerk's work, depends not on the nature of their labour but on how many people want it, and on how much they want it – that is to say, supply and demand.

Social democratic theory and social inequality

An altogether different approach to the question of whether and how inequality may be justified has been developed within what may loosely be termed the 'social democratic' tradition of thought. The key writer here is the American philosopher John Rawls who published his immensely influential *A Theory of Justice* in 1972.

Rawls approaches the question of social justice by asking what criteria of distribution people would come up with if they had to devise a social system without knowing what place they would occupy within it. His answer is first, that in this 'original position' of absolute ignorance, we would all agree on a principle of equal liberties (that is, legal equality), and second, that we would also all agree on a system in which resources are allocated equally except where an unequal distribution could be shown to benefit those who end up with least. He terms this second criterion 'the difference principle'.

Rawls's logic is impeccable. Not knowing whether we were going to be born rulers or ruled, we would opt for a democratic constitution which secured equal liberties for all. Similarly, not knowing whether we would be rich or poor, we would want a society in which everybody has the same, although we would also recognise that there might be conditions in which, by giving someone more than the rest, everybody could become better off in such a way that even the least affluent would benefit. For example, it may be that limited inequalities are necessary in order to provide incentives for a few individuals to innovate or work harder and thereby improve the situation of others, and in such a situation, inequality would be considered legitimate by people in the original position.

Rawls himself describes the difference principle as 'strongly egalitarian' (1972: 76) since there is a presumption in favour of equality unless a case can be made out for allowing some inequality to emerge. However, some people have found in Rawls's book a justification for widespread inequalities! The problem is that it is extremely difficult to judge whether a given set of inequalities is actually necessary if the worst off are to benefit. According to Hayek, for example, capitalism is a dynamic system which continually raises everybody's standards of living, but this will only continue for as long as people are permitted to accumulate and retain whatever resources the market affords them. Inequality, in other words, is the price to be paid for growth. Commodities which are envied at one point in time as the luxuries owned by the few soon become taken for granted as commonplace items to which virtually everybody has access. The poor today are incomparably richer than the poor were just a few generations ago. As Samuel McCracken (quoted in Berger 1987: 42) suggests, 'The poor live in what would have been thought of in the pre-capitalist period as ill-maintained castles.' Although the poor would undoubtedly benefit in the short term from redistribution, Hayek maintains that they and everyone else would lose in the long term as the society and economy stagnated through the erosion of incentives. Hayek likens capitalist societies to a 'moving column'; there are always people at the front and people bringing up the rear, but the whole column is always moving forwards, and everyone benefits as a result. If this is indeed the case, then the application of Rawls's difference principle could presumably justify wide inequalities – which does not appear to be his intention.

The major problem with Rawls's argument, however, is not that its implications for social inequality are unclear (although they are), but that its starting assumptions are untenable. This criticism is developed forcibly by Robert Nozick whose book, *Anarchy, State and Utopia* has since its publication in 1974 represented a major statement of the neo-liberal approach to the question of inequality.

Neo-liberal theory and social inequality

Nozick takes issue with the whole idea of people in an original position making judgements about just distributions

48

from behind a veil of ignorance, and his criticism of Rawls is by extension a criticism of a vast range of work in the sociology of stratification. Essentially, his argument is that 'social justice' cannot be determined in terms of the distribution of resources, but has to be judged by whether or not people have established a legitimate right to the things they own. In itself, the fact that a small proportion of the population might own a large proportion of the country's wealth tells us nothing about whether this is just, for the key question is how did they get it? The existence of inequalities, even great inequalities, is irrelevant to considerations of social justice.

Nozick takes exception to the very notion of 'distribution' as implying that resources are simply lying around ready-made and it is up to a society to decide who should have them. In Rawls's approach, for example, the problem for people in the original position is how to distribute houses, health care, factories and so on, but this begs the question of where these things originated. Income and wealth are generated from somewhere by someone. A country's resources do not simply exist waiting to be distributed – they come into the world with claims already attached to them. These claims or entitlements are, according to Nozick, established by virtue of people making things and freely exchanging them. Justice, in other words, has nothing to do with patterns of distribution of goods (*end states*) but is established through entitlements to those goods (the *means* by which they are acquired). The idea that people's possessions, legitimately acquired, can be taken away and given to someone else is not a realisation of social justice but a negation of it.

Nozick agrees with Rawls that people in the original position as he describes it probably would opt for egalitarianism. He likens this to a group of students, none of whom has any idea how well or badly they may have done in an examination, all agreeing to accept a mark of 50 per cent. Yet such a notion is absurd when we realise that people are not obliged to make such judgements in ignorance. Students, for example, know how hard they have worked and how likely they are to get good marks, and those who feel they have done well would be most aggrieved were they to be stripped of 30 per cent of their marks in the name of social justice! The marks cannot simply be distributed, for each candidate has already established an entitlement to a particular grade. So it is with material resources. Provided we are entitled to them by virtue of our work and our participation in uncoerced exchanges with others, there is no more to be said, and the issue of whether we end up with more or less than someone else is irrelevant.

Nozick has provided a powerful critique of Rawls and of all distributional measures of social justice. But how well does his own argument stand up? There is one major problem with his entitlement theory, and that is that many people in a country like Britain seem to own things to which they are not entitled!

We saw earlier that British society emerged out of a long feudal period in which one class owned the land while others had no independent right to any land at all. Those who owned the land did so by grace of the monarch – originally, through the dispensations of William the Conqueror who gave out land to his Norman warlords who had helped him capture England, and subsequently through grants and favours by later kings and queens who rewarded their favourites with honours and estates. The origins of private land ownership in Britain, in other words, lie in force, conquest and patronage. Indeed, those who worked the land and made it fertile were precisely those who were deprived of owning it, and in a later period, even the land which remained in common ownership was expropriated through a series of Enclosure Acts. Later, of course, land changed hands freely through gifts and market transactions, but such free exchanges (which were legitimate in Nozick's terms) cannot establish just entitlement if the land had not itself originally been justly acquired (which it had not according to Nozick's principles).

Nozick is himself aware of this problem, so much so that he adds to his principles of just acquisition and just transfer a third principle of entitlement which he refers to as the rectification of injustice. This holds that, where resources have been acquired unjustly, the victims are entitled to full compensation (an example of this principle in practice would be the Australian Aborigines' claims for land rights on the grounds that their lands were forcibly taken from them at the time of European settlement). Yet if the principle of rectification is taken seriously, it effectively undermines the whole basis of modern-day property ownership in a country like Britain. At the very least it would seem to justify (nay, necessitate) the immediate expropriation of all the land held by such as the Duke of Westminster and the House of Windsor, and in all probability it would also justify the public ownership of all land given the impossibility of sorting out which individuals were originally entitled to which plots.

Nozick does not explore such possibilities, for it is clear that the problems posed by his principle of rectification are daunting. Just as Rawls has developed a theory which can be used to justify enormous inequalities which he was intent on opposing, so Nozick has developed a theory which would enable a dramatic redistribution of property despite his view that such a policy cannot be justified.

Despite the problems in each of these theories, they have important implications for the sociological analysis of stratification. In particular, we should be wary of assuming that inequality is necessarily immoral or socially damaging, for there are strong arguments to suggest that inequality is to some extent the price we pay for an expansion of a society's resources. We should also be alert to the problems entailed in any attempt to impose a 'just distribution' on a society, for redistribution can itself create injustice and there is no clear principle according to which people's 'just deserts' can be determined. To show that a society is unequal is by no means the same as showing that it is unfair.

Activities

1 A group of you are to play a game of Monopoly. Before you start, you all need to agree on the fair and just way of distributing the money at the start of the game. The rules say every player should receive £1,500 but you can devise a different rule provided everybody agrees.

Now start the game and play for twenty or thirty minutes. How much money and property does each player now have? What *now* do you consider to be a fair and just distribution? Which players would like to keep things as they are, and which would prefer a more equal share-out? What light, if any, does all this shed on the dispute between Rawls and Nozick?

2 In their survey on class in Britain, Marshall *et al.* asked their respondents, 'Do you think the distribution of income and wealth in Britain is a fair one?' How would you answer this question? How do you think a cross-section of the British public answered it? Do you think this is a neutral question or does it make implicit assumptions? What alternative question might a disciple of Nozick's have chosen to ask?

The universality of social inequality

We saw in the last section that some writers, such as Friedrich Hayek, argue that inequality is the necessary price to be paid for economic growth in market societies. In this view, individuals pursuing their own self-interest indirectly benefit everybody else at the same time as they benefit themselves. This is because, in a capitalist society, some individuals will try to make money by innovating, setting up businesses, or investing in other people's enterprises to enable them to expand. These risk-takers may fail, in which case they have to bear the costs themselves. But some of them will succeed by hitting upon a new venture which attracts customers. These successful entrepreneurs may well accumulate a fortune, but in doing so, they will have added to the productive power and wealth of the society as a whole. Not everybody will be able to afford the goods or services they produce, and most new commodities tend to be quite expensive at first. But over time, competitors will grow up who will also provide these or similar goods and services, and gradually, their price tends to fall and more and more people are able to buy them. Thus, a few entrepreneurs become rich, some others fail and go bust, and meanwhile the rest of society grows more affluent as it gains by their efforts.

It is not difficult to find examples to illustrate Hayek's argument. Motor cars, ballpoint pens, colour televisions, home computers, central heating systems, air travel – all are examples of goods which were not available, or were only available to a very few people, before the Second World War, yet which are now within reach of millions of ordinary people. It is Hayek's contention that such things may well not have been developed at all, and would certainly not have become widely available, were it not for the incentives offered in a capitalist society to those with talent and enterprise to use it in pursuit of material wealth. *Capitalism is dynamic because it is unequal*, and any attempt to equalise wealth and income will succeed only at the expense of stifling initiative, innovation and social and economic development.

Hayek's argument is specifically about modern capitalism. However, as we saw earlier, *all* human societies which have developed beyond simple hunting and gathering have been unequal societies, and these inequalities occur on all three dimensions of power identified by Weber. In other words, all these societies are characterised by inequality of material rewards, inequality of status and inequality in access to political power. State socialist societies may be less unequal in economic terms than most capitalist societies, yet they still exhibit considerable income differences. The ratio between the income of a factory manager and that of a manual worker in the Soviet Union is in the order of thirty to one, for example. Socialist societies are also hierarchically differentiated in terms of prestige just as capitalist societies are, although different kinds of social positions are sometimes ranked differently in each of the two systems. And political power is undeniably far more centralised and much less dispersed in the socialist societies than in the pluralistic democracies of the Western capitalist nations.

When we encounter a social phenomenon which appears to be universal across different kinds of societies at different periods in history, we are clearly justified in asking whether there is something inherent in social life which tends to produce it, even under widely different circumstances. The ubiquity of systems of social stratification thus inevitably poses the question of whether it is an inevitable feature of any social order. However, the sheer fact of the pervasiveness of systems of social stratification cannot of itself warrant the conclusion that social, economic and political inequality is inevitable or necessary. In this, as in all generalisations, we cannot assume that what has always occurred in the past will necessarily occur in the future. As societies change and develop, so new possibilities for social organisation may emerge. Evidence that social stratification is generalised across all societies we have known up until now is important but is not enough. What is needed in addition is some *explanation* of why this is. Put another way, only if we succeed in constructing a theory which shows that social stratification must arise in any society can we be justified in asserting that it is in some way necessary and hence unavoidable.

Socialist utopia and socialist reality

Marxist theory, of course, argues that social stratification is neither necessary nor inevitable. According to Marx, there will come a time when capitalism has developed as far as it possibly can. At this point, the wealth and productive capacity of capitalist societies will be enormous, so much so that a socialist revolution will be able to usher in a new kind of social organisation in which everybody's needs can be met. As he saw it, a future socialist society will be classless, for the productive assets will be owned in common rather than held by just one section of the population. Furthermore, there will be no need for inequalities of political power either, for the repressive power of the state is only needed in a society where one class has to prevent another from threatening its privileges. Collective decisions in a socialist society would be made by delegates, elected by workers and instantly replaceable if they tried to do anything which the majority of workers did not like.

One response to this theory, of course, is to show that, where socialism has been tried, it has not resulted in a classless and politically equal social order. In countries like China and the Soviet Union, the major productive resources are owned by the state, but this is not the same thing as being owned in common. Large state bureaucracies have developed to manage these assets, and top bureaucrats and party officials have, in the view of many commentators, come to constitute a 'new class' which pays itself handsomely, claims high prestige by living in the best areas and driving around in chaffeur-driven limousines, and which is strongly resistant to popular demands and opinions.

Many Marxists respond to such observations by recognising their empirical validity but denying that this represents a refutation of Marx's theory. Socialism, they point out, was meant to develop in the most advanced capitalist countries. It is therefore not a fair test to point to countries like the Soviet Union or China, for these were very backward economies when they had their revolutions, and they therefore lacked the wealth to enable a truly socialist order to emerge. For these writers, Marx's propositions have yet to be properly tested, and we must wait for a socialist transformation in an advanced capitalist society before we can judge their truth or falsity.

This response is far from satisfactory, for as Peter Berger (1987) points out, we should analyse any type of society, capitalist or socialist, by looking at existing examples rather than by positing idealised utopias. Every socialist regime which has hitherto existed has failed to come near to Marxist expectations. Each new socialist country seems to enjoy a short honeymoon period with Marxist sympathisers before they are forced to admit that it has 'gone wrong' in some way, just as all its predecessors did. In the 1930s, Western Marxists thought that the Soviet Union represented their ideal. When the story of Stalin's purges came to light, sympathies ebbed away and a new generation of Marxists came to place their faith in China instead. The horrors of the Cultural Revolution finally convinced most of the error of this judgement, following which Cuba, or Kampuchea, or Tanzania, or Nicaragua has risen to prominence, only to become discredited as evidence of bloodshed, persecution, privilege or corruption has come to light. Something like a third of the world's population now lives under regimes which rule in the name of Marxism, yet none of them have realised the promise of Marx's writings. A critical sociology informed by comparative empirical evidence might be expected to conclude from this that there is something in the Marxist project itself which makes things 'go wrong'.

Evidence that socialist countries are still very unequal and are usually also highly repressive may lead us to question Marx's theory, but it still does not necessarily mean that stratification is inevitable. Is it not possible that some society will emerge at some later date where economic, social and political inequalities have more or less disappeared? To answer this, we need to turn to social theory, and in particular to the American functionalist tradition.

Functionalist explanations for social inequality

Functionalist theory attempts to explain the existence and persistence of social phenomena by identifying the positive effects they have for the social systems in which they occur. Seen in this light, it might seem odd that stratification should have become a focus for functionalist theories, for inequalities clearly have a number of negative effects in a society like modern Britain. Inequalities produce resentment and jealousy which, in extreme form, can boil over into open conflicts. They also represent blockages to the emergence of talent and enterprise insofar as wealthy or powerful groups may try to reserve their privileges for themselves and prevent others from rising to positions of responsibility and eminence. Furthermore, the existence of inequalities may result in fatalism on the part of the less privileged strata who are therefore unlikely to give of their best or to participate actively in social life. Such considerations suggest that systems of stratification are *dysfunctional* rather than functional for a society – a point made forcibly by Melvin Tumin (1953), among others.

However, it does not follow that, if a phenomenon has some negative social consequences, it does not also perform a valuable, positive and even necessary function. The existence of a system of social stratification may well generate conflict and inhibit the best use of available talent, but it could be that these are the price that has to be paid for the realisation of other, more important objectives.

The paper which first explicitly set out the argument that stratification does indeed represent a functional and necessary element of any social system was originally published by Kingsley Davis and Wilbert Moore in 1945. They argued, not only that all human societies are stratified, but also that this is necessarily the case since stratification meets a need which all societies have to confront: namely, the problem of how to motivate people to occupy key positions and to perform the duties required of these positions. 'Social inequality,' they say, 'is an unconsciously evolved device by which societies ensure that the most important positions are conscientiously filled by the most qualified persons' (Davis and Moore 1966: 48).

Davis and Moore recognised that different kinds of positions will be more or less important in different kinds of societies. While recognising that it is not always easy to determine precisely which positions are the most important for a society's survival and wellbeing, Davis and Moore suggested that in general, the most important positions are those which are to a large extent unique (in other words, other positions cannot substitute for what they do), and/or those on which a large number of other positions depend. In our own society, for example, the position of company managers is more important than that of floor sweepers. Both groups, of course, are indispensable, but managers are 'more unique' (for they could do the cleaning, but cleaners could not manage the firm) and they have more subordinate positions depending upon them (in that their decisions affect what many other people in the firm are able to do).

The functional importance of a position is one factor which determines its ranking in the system of stratification. The other is the amount of talent and training which is required for the duties of that position to be discharged adequately. Thus managers need entrepreneurial flair, skills in planning complex organisations, a high level of numeracy and literacy, and so on. Sweepers, on the other hand, need little natural talent and require only basic education and training.

According to Davis and Moore, functionally important positions will tend to be rewarded highly – both in terms of material resources and prestige – because any society must ensure that the most appropriate people are encouraged to take up the most important positions. If a position is important, it must be filled, and this often means that the rewards must be made attractive.

By the same logic, positions requiring extensive training or scarce talents will also tend to be highly rewarded so as to ensure that talented people do not waste their abilities in a less demanding position, and that enough people are willing to subject themselves to the years of education and training necessary for these positions to be filled.

It follows from all of this that stratification is universal precisely because systems of unequal reward are necessary. In a truly equal society, there would be no mechanism which could guarantee that the most important positions were filled (for people would have no incentive to take them), nor would there be any way of ensuring that people in these positions were motivated to perform at the best of their ability (for their rewards would be no higher than if they lazed around all day doing nothing).

Activities

1 Earlier in this chapter you were invited to play a game of Monopoly. Did anybody want to be banker? If not, how was a banker chosen or selected? Did the most appropriate person (for example, the best mathematician or the most honest player) end up doing it? If not, how might a better person have been encouraged to take on the task?

2 If you are a member of a school, college or evening class, try to organise a very short survey in which you ask fellow students who are over sixteen and who are taking various different courses why they have decided to continue with their studies. How many say it is to secure a better income later on (in other words, to improve their prospects)? Ask your respondents whether they would still pursue their studies if they were told that additional qualifications would bring no extra financial reward. What is the significance of your findings as regards the Davis and Moore thesis?

The debate over the Davis–Moore thesis

The Davis and Moore thesis has over the years been subjected to a barrage of criticisms. Among the most important are:

1. The theory does not fit most pre-industrial societies where positions are ascribed by birth.

We saw earlier, for example, that in the Indian caste system, certain positions are reserved for certain castes and that it is impossible for people to change their caste. Similarly in feudal Europe, top positions were effectively monopolised by members of royal and aristocratic families. Are we to believe that this tight system of exclusion was functional and necessary for the survival of these societies? Certainly there was little chance of talented people from lower strata rising to fill the most important positions.

In his response to this objection, Kingsley Davis claimed that the theory had been misunderstood. The theory does not claim that every society must attract the best people into the key positions (this would be tantamount to saying that every society must be meritocratic, which is clearly absurd). Rather, the argument is that top positions must be rewarded well enough to ensure that they are adequately filled and that those who occupy them are motivated to perform their tasks properly. In feudal Europe, for example, many members of the noble families were more interested in hunting or banqueting or travelling than they were in running the country. Like every other society, therefore, feudal society had to develop a system of rewards to attract people (from among those deemed eligible) to give up these pleasures and accept key positions. The key point here is that the functionalist theory of stratification has never claimed to explain why certain individuals come to occupy certain positions (which is how the critics have often interpreted it). Rather, it seeks to show why some positions are rewarded more highly than others – that is, why different social strata develop and persist. The focus is on the hierarchy of positions, not on the people who fill them.

2. *The assessment of functional importance is no more than a value judgement.*

It is impossible to say that any one position is more important than any other. There are two points here. First, all positions in society are functionally important, otherwise they would not exist. Sweepers are important, just as managers are, and the judgement that one is more important than the other is entirely a subjective point of view. Second, while it may be conceded that some positions have greater importance by virtue of others depending upon them, this logic only works within specific types of organisation and does not allow us to compare across organisations. For example, we may accept that the manager is more important than the person who sweeps the floor, just as we may accept that a doctor is more important than the nurse who holds the swab in the operating theatre. But on what possible grounds can we determine the relative importance of the manager and the doctor, or that of the sweeper and the nurse? Their functions are entirely different and thus non-comparable.

Davis's response to this is to point out that societies and social groups very often distinguish more or less important decisions. During the Second World War, for example, some occupations were 'reserved', and those working in them were not conscripted into the armed forces precisely because these particular positions were deemed to be more vital to Britain's survival than others. Similarly, governments and private organisations constantly make decisions about how scarce resources should be allocated among different tasks. The criteria of importance which he and Wilbert Moore identified were 'clues' to guide us in discriminating between positions of differing importance, and there may presumably be other equally useful or better criteria which could be developed. But to say that the whole notion of functional importance is based on a subjective value judgement is ridiculous, for it is apparent that societies themselves draw such distinctions all the time.

3. *There is an implicit conception of 'human nature' in this theory which is untenable.*

Davis and Moore were Americans who assumed that the culture of American capitalism is in some way universal. It may be true in the USA that people have to be offered material and other incentives before they will enter key positions or perform to the best of their ability, but this may not be true of other countries. Is it not at least plausible to suppose, even in the USA, that people may be motivated by factors such as the intrinsic satisfaction to be derived from doing a responsible job, or by a sense of 'social duty' and altruism? The theory assumes that human beings are always driven by self-interest and that they will lapse into sloth unless stimulated by the offer of incentives, but this assumption is at best unprovable, and at worst disproved by evidence from other cultures.

Davis accepts that people are not always motivated by self-interest. However, he also points out that no society can risk relying entirely on other motives. Intrinsic job satisfaction, for example, is an important reward for some people, but not all the positions that need to be filled in a society are inherently enjoyable. If we all did exactly what we most enjoyed, many key positions would go unfilled. Marx once suggested that under socialism, people could choose to hunt in the morning, fish in the afternoon and read books in the evening, but he never explained who was going to maintain the stock of deer, manufacture the fishing rods and harvest the forests for the paper mills. Not surprisingly, socialist societies modelling themselves on Marx's writings have generally found that extra incentives are needed to fill the less enjoyable positions, which is exactly what Davis and Moore would have predicted.

Similarly, people may well be motivated by a sense of service and public duty, but we cannot rely on such goodwill and altruism. We have all experienced group situations where something needs to be done yet nobody is willing to volunteer to do it. Besides, says Davis, even altruism needs rewarding. Few of us have the patience and commitment of Boxer, the horse in George Orwell's *Animal Farm* who took on all the tasks and never once looked for recognition. When we make sacrifices for the good of others, we often need to feel that our virtue has been recognised in some tangible way. For Davis, then, the joy of work and a sense of social service are important motives in human affairs, but they supplement reward mechanisms and cannot substitute for them.

4. *The idea that training is a sacrifice which has to be rewarded is little more than a rationalisation.*

Top income groups in our society often claim that their incomes can be justified with reference to all the hard work which they did in getting to these positions. This idea is reflected in the Davis and Moore theory which asserts that unequal rewards are necessary in order to encourage people to go in for the lengthy periods of training required before key positions can be filled. Yet training is rarely a real hardship, for the student life can be extremely enjoyable, and there is no reason to believe that training will always and necessarily be experienced as a sacrifice. Furthermore, any loss of earnings incurred in the period of training – both in the sense of income foregone and the actual cost of courses – is very swiftly made up. Tumin (1966), for example, shows that in the USA, the accumulated earnings of highly educated groups catch up with those of untrained workers within ten years of entering the workforce, and for the next twenty or thirty years, the gap in earnings stretches wider and wider.

Davis totally rejects these arguments. Studying, he claims, is experienced by many as a burden, and large numbers of young people are unwilling to undertake it. In Britain today, for example, there is a desperate shortage of graduate engineers, yet despite increased numbers of university places on engineering degrees, students are not applying to take these courses. If the Davis and Moore thesis is correct, more inducements are needed to encourage eighteen-year-olds to apply for these courses and to undertake three years' training which most are reluctant to do. The fact that highly trained people swiftly make up their loss of earnings once they enter the labour market does not mean that training is not a sacrifice. Indeed, such evidence supports the theory rather than refuting it! It is precisely because training is a sacrifice that our society finds it necessary to offer high rewards to those who complete it. In the case of engineering, for example, it seems clear that career prospects need to be made even more attractive than they are if sufficient numbers of suitably able and trained people are to fill the vacancies in the future.

An evaluation of the functionalist theory of stratification

The debate over the issues raised by the functionalist theory of stratification rumbled on for some years, particularly in the USA. By the mid-1960s, however, the debate seemed to run out of steam. As is so often the case in sociology, argument was met with counter-argument and few people on either side seemed very impressed by the case put by their opponents. During the 1960s, functionalist theory itself fell out of fashion as phenomenological and Marxist approaches seized the imagination of a new generation of scholars. The Davis and Moore thesis was never really refuted; it was simply pushed aside as sociologists turned to other more novel concerns.

The arguments developed by Davis and Moore are, however, crucial to any consideration of social stratification. Even their critics accepted their starting premiss – that all societies appear to have been stratified. Melvin Tumin opened his well-known critique, for example, by recognising that, 'The fact of social inequality in human society is marked by its ubiquity and its antiquity. Every known society, past and present, distributes its scarce and demanded goods and services unequally' (Tumin 1966: 53). Where Tumin and other critics parted company with Davis and Moore was over the explanation and implications of this fact.

The argument really boils down to two simple questions. First, do stratification systems perform positive functions in human societies? Second, if they do, does this explain their existence and does it mean that stratification is therefore inevitable?

On the first question, it seems that systems of stratification can be shown to have beneficial effects, although they may also have detrimental effects at the same time. The most sensible conclusion we can draw on this is that a system which rewards different positions unequally does have certain positive effects, although this does not mean that the same effects could not be achieved in some other way. As Robert Merton (1949) showed in his reformulation of functionalism, the fact that something performs positive functions for a society does not rule out the possibility that it may also be dysfunctional, nor that there may be functional alternatives to it. In other words, to show that something is functional is not to demonstrate that it is necessary.

This brings us to the second question, for clearly Davis and Moore did not succeed in demonstrating the necessity or inevitability of social stratification. They did show that systems of stratification are *one* way in which the social problem of filling the key positions and motivating those who occupy them may be met, but they did not show that this is the *only* way in which this could be accomplished.

It is possible to imagine a society where all positions are rewarded equally in terms of material resources and formal status. The question then is how these positions would be filled. The only answer is that some powerful authority would be required which could cajole, and if need be coerce, people into certain positions and which could police them sufficiently to ensure that they continued to perform their duties properly. This is not to deny that some people – perhaps a majority – would be happy to go where they were needed and to work as hard as they could. But Davis was correct to say that no system could rely entirely on mobilising such altruistic sentiments, for the problem would inevitably arise of what to do about those individuals who refused to go where they were needed, or who failed to perform their tasks adequately. In the absence of economic rewards and penalties, the only sanctions available would be those involving the threat or use of physical force. Such people, in other words, would have to be jailed, or forcibly set to work in supervised colonies, or even executed as an example to the others. Indeed, the use of force and close surveillance in such a society would inevitably escalate, for not only would some people try to resist being told what to do, but evasion would become a major problem. 'Economic crimes' would become a significant threat to the whole social order, for if some people got away with doing less or taking more than their share, this would erode the commitment of everybody else. Such 'criminals' would doubtless need to be dealt with very harshly, just as those guilty of 'economic crimes' in China are today publicly executed in front of crowds of thousands.

Social stratification, then, is not the only way of allocating people to positions in society. Coercion, repression and terror could achieve the same objective, possibly just as effectively. But these are the only two feasible ways in which this problem could be met. As the American neo-liberal economist Milton Friedman argues, 'Fundamentally, there are only two ways of coordinating the economic activities of millions. One is central direction involving the use of coercion – the technique of the army and of the modern totalitarian state. The other is voluntary cooperation of individuals – the technique of the market place' (Friedman 1962: 13).

It is probably true to say that all societies rely on some mixture of both these techniques, although contemporary capitalist societies rely more than most on material induce-ments and have not normally had to resort overmuch to physical force, except in times of war and national emergency when labour has been drafted. As a result, capitalist countries often turn out to be more unequal (in terms of the distribution of economic resources) than socialist ones, but socialist countries are always more repressive. To the extent that socialist countries such as China and the Soviet Union have begun to move more towards the use of markets and economic incentives, their reliance on state coercion may be expected to decline.

Max Weber argued that sociology cannot dictate our values; we must decide for ourselves what is good and what is bad. It is therefore for each of us to judge the respective merits of a system based mainly on material inducements and a system based mainly on physical force. However, Weber did see that sociology can help us make moral judgements by informing us of the likely implications of pursuing particular values. In this section, we have seen that the value of egalitarianism is not necessarily unattainable, but it could only be realised at the price of individual liberty. Equality and liberty are incompatible objectives. If we desire one, we must sacrifice the other. We have, therefore, to choose between these values, for it is a major contribution of modern sociology to have recognised that we cannot have both.

Further reading

Marx's views on income distribution and the principle of allocation of resources in a socialist or communist society are most succinctly set out in his 'Critique of the Gotha programme', reprinted in Marx and Engels (1968) Selected Works, London: Lawrence & Wishart. There is a large secondary literature on Rawls, and much of it is heavy going, but a helpful discussion of his ideas can be found in K. Carey (ed.) (1985) 'Unveiling the right', Tawney Society — see especially the introduction and chs. 2 and 3. If you attempt Rawls in the original, concentrate on sections 1–4, 10–30, 34 and 39. The key section of Nozick's book is Part Two (which includes the critique of Rawls). A useful left-wing critique of Nozick is provided by G. Cohen (1985) 'Nozick on appropriation', New Left Review 150, while David Green's (1987) The New Right, Brighton: Wheatsheaf, provides a more sympathetic account of his ideas in chapter 2. The main contributions to the debate over the functionalist theory of stratification are collected together in R. Bendix and S. Lipset (eds) (1967) Class, Status and Power, London: Routledge & Kegan Paul.

4

Social mobility

Social mobility in industrial societies

The Davis and Moore thesis was concerned solely with the question of why different positions in society come to be ranked and rewarded differently. They deliberately did not address the related question of why particular individuals come to find themselves in specific social positions. It is to this issue that we now turn.

Trends in social mobility

We have already seen that systems of stratification based on social class tend to be more 'open' than those based on status. What this means is that people's position in modern class societies is not determined at birth in the way that it tended to be in feudal and caste systems. There is movement between class positions. This movement may occur within one individual's lifetime (for example, the person who starts work as a clerk and ends up as managing director), in which case sociologists refer to *intra-generational mobility*. Or movement may occur between generations as children achieve a different position from that occupied by their parents, in which case we refer to *inter-generational mobility*.

It is also an important feature of class systems that movement between classes may occur in both directions. It is possible, for example, to start life as the son of a petrol pump attendant but end up as a chartered accountant, just as it is also possible for the daughter of a high court judge to end up as a shorthand typist. In other words, movement may involve both *upward mobility* and *downward mobility*.

Three points can immediately be made about the pattern of social mobility in all industrial societies. The first is that rates of inter-generational mobility have generally become more significant over time. It is now far more common than it used to be for children to enter the workforce at a much higher position than their parents attained when they started work. The reason for this is that all industrial countries have come to place greater emphasis on formal qualifications, and most have expanded educational provisions over the last fifty years. It is therefore now easier for working-class children to gain qualifications before entering work. Whether it has at the same time become more difficult to 'work one's way up' from an initial lowly position is a matter of some dispute. Some observers argue that what the working class has gained on the inter-generational mobility swings, it has lost on the intra-generational mobility roundabouts, but as we shall see below, there is little evidence to back up such assertions.

The second point is that upward social mobility is more common than movement downwards. The reason for this is that technological change and the shift in employment from industry to services has expanded the number of higher positions while demand for unskilled manual labour has declined. Each generation finds that there are more high-status jobs available than was the case when its parents left school, and some degree of upward mobility is thus inevitable.

For this reason, the mere existence of upward mobility does not necessarily indicate that a class system is open and meritocratic. Sociologists have often insisted that rates of downward mobility are therefore a better indicator of the openness of a system, for evidence of movement downwards indicates an inability of upper strata to maintain their privileges in the face of competition from below.

The third point is that movement across a short range of positions in the social hierarchy is more common than movement across a wide range. This is not surprising, of course, for we should expect individuals to find it easier to improve their position marginally than to improve it dramatically.

Measuring social mobility

This third point raises a fundamental problem in the study of social mobility, however, for it is not always clear that marginal changes in position really constitute social mobility at all. For example, many studies have shown considerable movement across the boundary between manual and non-manual occupations. This is especially marked in the case of women, for many typically female occupations are classified as routine white collar jobs (secretaries, clerks, personal service workers, and so on). But if the daughter of a skilled fitter leaves school with a handful of mediocre GCSE certificates and gets employment as a filing clerk, does this really represent upward movement? Her wages may never reach the earnings of her father, her responsibility and authority is minimal, and her status is fairly low despite the fact that she does her work in skirt and blouse rather than overalls.

It follows from this that any analysis of social mobility must remain alert to three related issues. First, we must not allow ourselves to be misled by statistics showing large-scale movements across very narrow ranges, for in many cases, such changes may be virtually insignificant as regards people's life chances, life styles and self-conceptions. Second, we must constantly bear in mind that social stratification is multi-dimensional, and that a move upwards on one dimension (an improvement in social status, for example) need not imply a simultaneous move upwards on others (an increase in authority or a rise in income, for example). And third, we need to bear in mind that people's lives often follow very 'lumpy' trajectories – our hypothetical female filing clerk, for example, may leave work after a few years, have children, and move back into a very different occupation in middle age. Comparison of people's positions at one point in time may therefore ignore important changes which occur in other periods of their lives.

Making comparisons

Because the measurement of social mobility is so notoriously difficult, disagreements abound in sociology about its extent and its significance. This is particularly the case in respect of international comparisons of social mobility rates in different countries, for here there is the added complication that similar positions may be ranked differently in different societies! As regards the prestige which is typically accorded to different occupations, a classic study by Inkeles and Rossi (1956) showed that, although there is quite high agreement between people in different industrial countries over the desirability of most occupations, there are also some specific and noticeable differences. Manual work, for example, is more highly regarded by people in the Soviet Union than it is in Britain or the USA, and Lane (1982) has shown that skilled manual jobs are consistently ranked higher than junior non-manual jobs in socialist countries. Such variations may be reflected on other dimensions of stratification as well. Manual workers in the Soviet Union, for example, are on average paid more than routine non-manual workers. Given such differences, comparisons between East and West which focus on movements between manual and non-manual occupations (as most of them have done) would appear to be of limited use or validity.

71

Even within one country, however, evidence on social mobility rates has often been interpreted very differently by different sociologists according to the criteria they adopt for measuring it. An analysis which focuses on inter-generational upward mobility between manual and non-manual occupations is likely to conclude that the British class system is remarkably fluid and open. A different analysis which concentrates on intragenerational downward mobility between top and bottom strata is, by contrast, almost certain to conclude that the system is remarkably static and closed! Many children from manual working-class homes get white-collar jobs, but there are precious few examples of directors of large companies who end their lives sweeping the streets!

Social inequalities and natural inequalities

Before we come on to consider the evidence, one further point needs to be raised, and this concerns the vexed issue of natural abilities and cultural advantages. The problem is directly posed by the example we have just considered. Suppose we find very low rates of substantial downward mobility in a society – that is to say, most people in top positions stay there, and their children too generally maintain a position at least as high as that occupied by their parents. What are we to conclude from this? The evidence would not necessarily indicate social closure on the part of a privileged stratum, for it may be that the members and children of the upper strata have maintained their position as a result of success in open competition with members of other classes. Social mobility rates on their own can therefore tell us little about how open and meritocratic a society is. In addition, we need to know whether members of different classes enjoy different social and cultural advantages such that people of equivalent abilities who work equally hard nevertheless end up in different positions.

In his book *The Division of Labour in Society* (originally published in 1893), Emile Durkheim argued that industrial societies would never operate harmoniously until social inequalities came to reflect the distribution of natural inequalities. The problem is that even were we to achieve such a state, we should probably never know that we had reached it, for measurement of natural abilities and talents is fraught with difficulties. Aptitude and intelligence tests provide us with clues about people's innate abilities, but the findings are always clouded by cultural factors which it is almost impossible to control. There are long and unresolved arguments in social psychology about the extent to which IQ scores indicate differences in natural intelligence as opposed to cultural background. When we measure the IQ of working-class and middle-class children, for example, we usually find that the former score on average lower than the latter (although variations within each group are always far more extensive than those between them). But does this mean that the middle-class children are on average more intelligent or does it mean that they are culturally better equipped to answer questions set by middle-class psychologists?

Because it is impossible to reach a satisfactory answer to such questions, it is also impossible to determine whether, in Durkheim's terms, social inequalities are the product and reflection of natural ones. Nevertheless, the difficulties of measuring innate differences between people should not lead us to conclude that they are therefore irrelevant or even non-existent. Different people do have different talents and abilities, and recent discoveries in biochemistry have shown that far more features of personality and character are transmitted genetically from generation to generation than had previously been realised. The significance of this for the study of social mobility is that a relative lack of movement across wide spans in the occupational hierarchy may be due as much to genetic inheritance as to social closure. After all, in a perfect meritocracy, the most talented people would occupy the top positions, and *if* talent is to a large extent transmitted through genetic inheritance, it would not be surprising to find that most of their offspring come to occupy these positions as well.

Activity

Study the following figures which are taken from John Goldthorpe's survey of social mobility among over 10,000 men in England and Wales (Goldthorpe 1980: 44). Class I consists of higher-level professionals, administrators and managers; Class II is lower-grade professionals, technicians, managers and supervisors of non-manual employees; Class III is mainly clerical and service workers in non-manual occupations; Class IV is small business people; Class V is the blue collar elite – lower-grade technicians, foremen, and so on; Class VI is made up of skilled manual workers; and Class VII is made up of semi- and unskilled manual workers.

Table 4.1 *The relation between social class of fathers and social class of sons*

Father's class	Respondent's class (%)						
	I	II	III	IV	V	VI	VII
I	25	12	10	7	3	2	2
II	13	12	8	5	5	3	3
III	10	10	11	7	9	6	6
IV	10	12	10	27	9	7	8
V	13	14	13	12	17	12	10
VI	16	22	26	24	31	42	35
VII	12	17	23	18	27	28	37

Source: Goldthorpe mobility survey 1980

What percentage of Class I males has been recruited from the working class? What percentage of men whose fathers were in Classes I or II end up in manual working-class jobs? What do these figures tell us about upward mobility from the working class into the top positions, and downward mobility from these positions into the working class? In a pure meritocracy, what sorts of figures would you expect to find in columns I and VII? How much do the actual figures diverge from this? Do you think this divergence is best explained as the result of differences between the classes (for example, in intelligence and diligence) or as the product of class inequalities in the opportunities available?

Social mobility in contemporary Britain

Bearing in mind all the problems regarding the measurement and interpretation of social mobility data, let us consider what is probably the most reliable evidence we have in relation to Britain. This is material gathered by John Goldthorpe and his colleagues at the University of Oxford in the early 1970s through a survey of over 10,000 men in England and Wales between the ages of twenty and sixty-four. We briefly encountered this study earlier in this chapter when we looked at the social class schema developed by Goldthorpe in which he seeks to combine work and market situations into a single combined scale. In what follows we shall consider the evidence relating to mobility by comparing movements between the seven social classes (which, as we saw, can be collapsed into three main strata) outlined in the Goldthorpe scheme.

Goldthorpe's study concentrates on inter-generational mobility, although he found that for working-class men, intra-generational mobility was still more common as a route out of the working class. Thus, three-quarters of the sons of working-class males started work in working-class occupations, but one-third of these subsequently rose into higher class positions. Looking at those who made it into the salariat, many more did so by working their way up than by direct entry on the strength of qualifications earned at school or college.

Goldthorpe points out that these findings refute the claims of those who believe that inter-generational opportunities have expanded but that intra-generational opportunities have contracted (the so-called *counterbalance thesis*). Comparing older and younger age cohorts in his sample, he shows that it was no more difficult for the younger group to work its way up after starting in employment than it had been for the older group. Put another way, the younger group had enjoyed greater opportunities of upward mobility through education while retaining the same chances of upward mobility within employment. As Goldthorpe puts it, 'Over recent decades, an increase in direct entry to the higher levels of the class structure has occurred without there being any apparent decline in the chances of access via indirect routes' (Goldthorpe 1980: 57). Or to put it another way, working-class upward mobility has been increasing as a result of wider educational opportunities without any sign of more traditional avenues of advancement being closed off. The system has become more open.

Turning to his data on inter-generational mobility, Goldthorpe tests two further theories, both of which (like the counterbalance thesis) hold that the British class system is relatively rigid and closed. One of these is the *closure thesis* which has normally been advocated by Marxist theorists such as Tom Bottomore and Ralph Miliband. This thesis suggests that social mobility is always limited to a short range and that top positions are virtually immune to its effects. Like the counterbalance thesis, however, this argument is refuted by Goldthorpe's evidence. Looking at entry into Class I (higher grade professionals and administrators plus managers and proprietors of large enterprises), he shows that only one-quarter of men in this class were born into it, and that over a quarter had come from manual working-class backgrounds. Rather than being closed off to the lower classes, this top class therefore 'displays, on any reckoning, a very wide basis of recruitment and a very low degree of homogeneity in its composition' (Goldthorpe: 43).

Nor does the *buffer zone thesis* fare any better! This theory holds that most movement is limited to the skilled manual and routine clerical grades who often change places with each other but who rarely move much higher or much lower in the system. Against this, Goldthorpe shows that 7 per cent of the sons of working-class fathers are now in Class I, and that a further 9 per cent are in Class II (lower-grade professionals and administrators, managers of small businesses, higher grade technicians and supervisors of non-manual employees). Furthermore, 15 per cent of the sons of Class I and II fathers are now in the manual working class.

These may not be staggeringly high figures, but they are large enough to refute any suggestion that long-range mobility is in any sense rare. Furthermore, although Goldthorpe himself believes that the high rate of working- and lower middle-class recruitment into Class I can be explained by the growth in size of the service class in recent decades (a trend we discuss in the next section), it is important to bear in mind the relatively high rates of *downward mobility* out of Classes I and II, and in particular into the working class. These figures cannot be explained by changes in the occupational structure but have to be accepted as evidence of a relatively open class system.

Very rarely have sociologists accepted the possibility that Britain might be a fairly open society, yet this is the direction in which the evidence points us. This does not mean that Britain is a meritocratic society, for relatively high rates of social mobility are not the same thing as equality of opportunity. It would be fatuous to assert that all individuals born into this country have the same opportunities. The black girl born of working-class parents who attends a large inner-city comprehensive school confronts far more disadvantages in terms of her cultural inheritance (what Bourdieu terms 'cultural capital') and barriers of racial, gender and class exclusivity than does the white boy born of upper-class parents who attends an expensive public school. The latter starts life with an enormous advantage. Yet having said that, it would be just as fatuous to conclude from this that Britain is a closed society in which a dominant class perpetuates itself while excluding others from its privileges. Sixteen per cent of males born into the working class make it to professional, managerial and administrative positions, and 15 per cent of males born into these top classes move in the opposite direction and end up in manual occupations. This is evidence of considerable fluidity and movement across the whole range of the occupational scale.

The pattern of increasing opportunities for upward mobility which Goldthorpe documented in the early 1970s seems to have continued in the years since then. Despite the slow-down in economic growth since the mid-seventies, Goldthorpe found a similar pattern from survey evidence collected in 1983 as he found in 1972. Indeed, if anything, the class system had become even more fluid. Thus, while 16 per cent of men of working-class origins had reached Classes I and II in 1972, this figure had risen to 24 per cent by 1983. Similarly, the proportion of working-class people who had working-class parents fell in these eleven years from 60 per cent to 53 per cent (in other words, the working class was recruiting more people than before from higher social classes). Clearly, while working-class children start life at a disadvantage, substantial numbers of them manage to overcome the obstacles and achieve significant upward mobility, although in the late 1980s, the penalty for failure may be higher than in the past, given the high rates of working-class unemployment.

Activity
Take a piece of paper and write down (where appropriate) your own occupation or intended occupation; your father's, mother's, grandfathers' and grandmothers' occupations; the occupations of your brothers and sisters; and the occupations of your adult children if you have any. If you have a copy of the OPCS *Classification of Occupations*, code each person to a social class; if you do not, then you will have to make your own judgement about which of the six Registrar-General classes each person probably belongs to.

How much evidence is there of upward or downward inter-generational social mobility in your family? Has there been much movement across large social distances or has most been short range? If you are in a school or college, try pooling your findings with others and work out percentage rates of mobility.

Note: You will have to make some crucial judgements about how to analyse your data. In particular, you need to think about what to do with households where the husband is in one class and the wife is in another – whose class will you take as the basis for comparison? You should also consider whether, in the case of your parents for example, it makes sense to look at their present occupation or the job they were in when they were your age. And how are you going to classify people who are retired, unemployed, housewives, students, etc.? The analysis of social mobility is fraught with difficulties!

How open is the British class system?

The previous section has outlined the evidence on social mobility in Britain. The puzzle is why this evidence has not led to a substantial revision in the image that so many sociologists and political commentators continue to portray of class in modern Britain. The stereotype of the British class system which is still reproduced in so many textbooks and articles is one of a rigid, closed and elitist order in which working-class talent is frustrated and squandered by the bucketful while a ponderous and incompetent ruling class holds on to the reins of economic power and leads us all further down the path to stagnation and ruin. As Bauer observes,

> It has become part of contemporary political folklore that a restrictive and divisive class system, almost a caste system, is the bane of this country. The system is supposed to be a major barrier to economic progress in Britain and also a

significant source of justified social discontent. This is
untrue.

(Bauer 1978: 1)

Whatever the reasons, however, the myth survives.

John Goldthorpe, for example, was apparently surprised by
his own findings (one of the delights of empirical sociology is
that its results can so often surprise us). But rather than
celebrate this evidence that the British class structure is more
open and fluid than he had imagined, and that social mobility
rates have increased over the years, Goldthorpe moved the
goalposts. His evidence, he claimed, showed only that
absolute rates of mobility had increased. He then set about
calculating what he termed *relative* rates which refer to the
chances of individuals in different classes ending up in higher
class positions than they start from.

On this relative measure, he found that there had been little
change. In other words, the system has become more open,
but the improved chances of mobility have been shared
equally by members of different social classes. Put another
way, the working class now has greater opportunities for
upward mobility than it used to, but so too do the classes
above it. Increased mobility has not favoured the working
class to any greater extent than other classes. On the strength
of this, Goldthorpe then triumphantly concludes that nothing
has really changed after all: 'No significant reduction in class
inequalities has in fact been achieved' (Goldthorpe 1980: 252).

This extraordinary line of reasoning has since been taken
up by other sociologists who are equally loath to believe that
the class system is not as rigid as they had hitherto supposed.
The recent Essex University survey, for example, found that
one-third of people in Classes I and II had started out in
Classes VI or VII, but the authors immediately emphasise
that, 'This upward mobility is not the result of changes in
relative mobility rates . . . There have been no changes in
social fluidity' (Marshall *et al.* 1988: 137). Like Goldthorpe,
they believe that nothing much has changed because, although

opportunities for working-class people have improved, so too have opportunities for middle-class people: 'More "room at the top" has not been accompanied by greater equality in the opportunities to get there' (Marshall *et al.* 1988: 138).

There are two major problems with this sort of argument. The first is its assumption that the only change worth talking about is one where top dogs lose, rather than one where everybody gains. The second is its assumption that everybody is equally capable of rising to fill the top positions in society.

The first of these assumptions exemplifies the taken-for-granted socialist–egalitarian political perspective which pervades so much of the sociological literature on stratification. For writers like Goldthorpe or the Essex team, capitalism is forever open to criticism no matter how much it improves people's living standards and opens up new opportunities for advancement and personal improvement, for capitalism always entails inequality between top and bottom. We saw earlier that neo-liberals such as Friedrich Hayek defend capitalism precisely on the grounds that, although it is an unequal system, it is also a dynamic one from which everybody benefits through economic expansion. This is an argument which is never considered in key works like those of Goldthorpe or Marshall and his colleagues, for they are concerned only with relativities and never with absolutes. It is as if a giant and a dwarf were to enter a hot air balloon. Where Hayek would celebrate their continuing ascent as beneficial to both of them, Goldthorpe and Marshall would continue to insist that nothing of any significance was going on since the giant was still nearer the clouds than the dwarf was.

Their commitment to a relativistic perspective sometimes leads these left-wing sociologists to make statements about British capitalism which are patently misleading. The Essex team, for example, conclude their discussion by asserting: 'The post-war project of creating in Britain a more open society, through economic expansion, educational reform and egalitarian social policies, has signally failed to secure its objectives' (Marshall *et al.* 1988: 138). Yet this is untrue, for

81

there are today many more opportunities for working-class people than there were before the war, and this is precisely because of one of the factors which they believe has been insignificant – namely, 'economic expansion'. The fact that the middle class has benefited too might better be seen as a bonus rather than as grounds for criticism.

The second problem with this sort of work is its implicit (though never stated) assumption that everybody has the same abilities, talents and aptitudes. What these authors do is to compare actual patterns of mobility with some perfect norm. According to this norm, people's starting point should have no effect on where they end up. Destinations in the class structure should therefore be randomly related to social origins. This criterion of perfect openness obviously assumes that genetic or natural advantages (including factors like differential parental support and encouragement) either do not exist or are randomly distributed between different social strata. It is an ideal which cannot admit of even the possibility that talents are unevenly distributed among people, that the most talented tend to rise towards the higher social positions, and that they tend to pass on some of their genetic advantages to some of their offspring. Like so many sociologists, Goldthorpe, Marshall and others simply rule out the possibility of different natural endowments and make an assumption in favour of entirely social explanations of patterns of inequality. Thus Goldthorpe bluntly states:

> Where inequalities in class chances of this magnitude can be displayed, *the presumption must be, we believe*, that to a substantial extent they do reflect inequalities of opportunity that are rooted in the class structure, and are not simply the outcome of the differential take-up of opportunities by individuals with differing genetic, moral or other endowments that do not derive from their class position.
>
> (Goldthorpe 1988: 252, emphasis added)

No justification is given for this 'presumption' and no attempt was made in the study to measure and compare the abilities and motivations of people who had been upwardly mobile with those who had not. So it is that sociology reproduces its own myths and continues to shut its ears and eyes to any development in psychology or molecular biology which might lead us at least to question this resolute commitment to social determinism.

Whereas Durkheim looked only for a society in which natural inequalities were reflected in social ones, Goldthorpe and many other contemporary sociologists effectively end up denying that such natural inequalities can have any importance in influencing people's destinies. If, for example, the working class accounts for half of the population, then for Goldthorpe and for the Essex researchers we should expect half of all doctors, managers and top civil servants to have originated in the working class. If we find, as Goldthorpe did, that only one quarter of such groups are from working-class origins, then according to this reasoning we are justified in assuming that the 'shortfall' is entirely due to social barriers and that British society is therefore just as class-ridden and unjust as its critics have always maintained. In the idealised world of John Goldthorpe and other 'left' sociologists, people's destinies should be randomly determined because talents are randomly distributed. British society is thus found wanting because people of working-class origins are not in the majority in all the top jobs. The argument is ludicrous, yet in modern sociology it is all too rarely questioned.

Further reading

Obviously the main source is Goldthorpe's Social Mobility and Class Structure in Modern Britain — *the new revised edition includes later data from a 1983 survey. A readable, though uncritical, discussion of the results of Goldthorpe's survey can be found in ch. 6 of A. H. Halsey (1986)* Change in British Society, *Oxford and New York: Oxford University Press, 3rd edition. The edited collection by A. Coxon and C. Jones (1975)* Social Mobility, *Harmondsworth: Penguin*

Books contains many of the classic articles by Miller, Blau and Duncan *on problems of measuring social mobility. For a critical (though empirically lightweight) attack on the view that Britain is a closed, class-ridden society, see* P. Bauer (1978) Class on the Brain, *London: Centre for Policy Studies.*

5

The changing class system in Britain

The fragmented class structure

We saw in the last chapter that one factor which explains relatively high rates of upward mobility is the expansion of the service class and the contraction of the manual working class. This same factor, of course, makes evidence of continuing downward mobility all the more remarkable. Nevertheless, it should alert us to the fact that, when analysing the British class structure, we are aiming at a moving target. It is not just that individuals change position within the system, for the system too is changing.

Compared with the nineteenth century, when Marx developed his theory, the class system has become highly complex and differentiated. Technical change has reduced the size of the traditional proletariat and has opened up a wide range of new positions. Similarly, the increase in administration within both the private and public sectors has generated a need for managers and specialists on a scale undreamed of in Marx's day. Rather than polarising, as Marx believed it would, the class system seems to have fragmented, or at least to be undergoing fundamental restructuring. Old divisions seem to be fading in significance and new lines of cleavage are appearing.

The changes which have been occurring during the twentieth century, and more especially over recent decades, can be explored by considering what has happened at five different levels of the class system. Three of these – the middle class, the lower middle or 'intermediate' class, and the working class – correspond to the three basic categories of Goldthorpe's class schema. In addition, we also need to consider what has happened at the top, to the capitalist class, and at the very bottom, to the stratum which Marx referred to as the 'lumpenproletariat' and which some recent commentators have identified as the 'underclass'.

The capitalist class

Although Marx believed that the owners of capital were one of the two major classes in capitalist societies, even he recognised that changes were occurring towards the end of his life which were significantly altering the nature of this class. The key change was the development of the joint stock company.

The division of ownership and control

In the early days of modern capitalism, individuals or families set up businesses mainly using either their own wealth or money borrowed from merchants and (later) banks. By the second half of the nineteenth century, however, the market for manufactured goods was fast expanding on to a world scale and many firms began to grow very fast, both by increased investment and by take-overs and mergers. Such expansion required new sources of money, and the solution was normally found by offering shares to the public. What this meant was that members of the public would purchase a fraction of the company, in return for which they would receive a proportionate share in its profits. The company for its part was able to use the money raised by the sale of shares to invest in new plant, machinery or whatever.

Today, most large companies, and many smaller ones, are owned by a range of different shareholders. There is, in other words, no one identifiable capitalist owner. The thousands of different shareholders who together own a given company are entitled to attend a meeting each year where they vote on various aspects of company policy and elect a board of directors. If the company is doing badly, they may decide to elect new directors to replace the existing ones, or they may decide to accept a take-over bid from a competing board of another, more successful, competitor.

The significance of all this for a sociological analysis of stratification is that ownership of capital is now dispersed, while those who run these big companies – the top managers and directors – are not the people who own them. Ownership and control, in other words, have become separated. The nineteenth-century image of the capitalist entrepreneur running his (or occasionally her) own firm is not entirely anachronistic, for some sizeable concerns are still owned in large part by particular individuals or families, but the typical pattern today is that of a company run by a board of directors who are directly accountable to thousands of shareholders. This inevitably poses the question: Who and where is the capitalist class in Britain today?

Who owns capital today?

Two key points need to be made about the structure of ownership and control. The first concerns the directors and top managers, for it is not strictly true to say that they control enterprises but do not own them. Many directors own shares in their own (and in other) companies. Indeed, many directors also sit on the boards of several different companies – there is an interlocking network at the top of British industry and finance in which the same names and faces keep cropping up with different hats on.

This does not constitute a capitalist class in any meaningful sense of the word, for this group's ownership of capital still only accounts for a small fraction of the total (less than a quarter of the 250 largest companies are run by directors who own as much as 5 per cent of the shares), and its income is usually derived more from salaries than from revenue accruing through ownership of assets. Nor is it a 'ruling class' in the sense that Marx saw capitalists as a ruling class, for although these people are undoubtedly powerful in shaping economic investment decisions, they do not control the society as a whole and they are sometimes dismayed by the failure of governments, educationalists, the mass media and so on to defer to their wishes and interests. What this group represents is an influential economic elite, for in a situation where the one hundred largest companies now account for over half of all manufacturing output in Britain, it is clear that a few thousand individuals at most are today responsible for taking the bulk of the key financial and administrative decisions which shape the future development of British industry and banking.

The second point concerns the pattern of share ownership. Ownership of shares by individuals steadily declined in Britain up to 1980. In 1958, 7 per cent of the population owned shares, but by 1979, this had declined to just 4.5 per cent. Since then, government policies of privatising companies such as British Gas, British Telecom and British Airways has dramatically raised this proportion. In 1987, a survey conducted for the OPCS indicated a likely figure of around 19 per cent, although the majority of these new shareholders own shares in only one company and half of them have total share assets worth less than £1,000. The privatisation sales have perhaps been most significant in boosting employee shareholding, for nineteen in every twenty workers in British Telecom, British Gas, British Airways and Rolls Royce bought shares, and most of them have kept them. This, of course, further complicates the class division between 'capital' and 'labour', for in many companies today, labour owns part of the capital!

The most important point about shareholding, however, is that, notwithstanding the recent rise in the numbers of individuals who own shares, most shares are today owned by large financial institutions. In 1963, over half of all shares were personally owned and insurance companies, pension funds and unit trusts owned just 18 per cent. Just twelve years later, personal and institutional holdings matched each other at 38 per cent. Since then, the institutions have continued to increase their relative holdings.

The significance of this trend cannot be overestimated. Around half of the British population now belongs to private pension schemes, for example. Every month, they pay into a pension fund, and the managers of the fund invest this money in shares or any other asset which they believe will show a good long-term return. Similarly, millions of ordinary people pay regular life insurance premiums, and millions more buy their homes with endowment mortgages, and their payments too are invested by insurance managers in shares and other assets. Some people buy unit trusts. In this case, the managers of the trust buy and sell shares, and dividends are paid on the aggregate profit they make from the entire portfolio. And most recently, the government has backed Personal Equity Plans under which individuals invest in small parcels of shares and enjoy tax privileges on the dividends and capital gains they receive.

What all this means is that, although direct ownership of capital is not widespread (for the majority of personal shareholdings are still concentrated in a small number of hands), indirect ownership is remarkably diffused. All those millions of people who pay their monthly pension contributions, insurance premiums, endowment mortgages or whatever probably do not even know how their money is being invested, and they certainly have precious little say about it, but their future and economic security is intimately bound up with the profits made by capitalist enterprises in Britain and abroad. They may well be workers, but taken together, they are also the people who own the great bulk of the capital in this country.

The end of the capitalist class?

What, then, of the capitalist class? There are still a few examples of old capitalist families who have hung on to a majority holding in their companies, and there are some new entrepreneurs who have set up successful enterprises from which they have made millions. There is also still a traditional landowning class, although even here, increasing amounts of land are being bought as an investment by the financial institutions. The basic point, however, is that the financial structure of modern capitalism is one where it is increasingly difficult to identify a specific capitalist class. The people who run the economy only own a tiny fraction of the total assets. The people who work in it very often have a direct or indirect investment in its continued profitability.

Ever since the 1930s, sociologists have been suggesting that these developments may have profound social implications. In his *Capitalism, Socialism and Democracy*, first published in 1943, Joseph Schumpeter forecast the end of capitalism on the grounds that the old-style innovative entrepreneur was being replaced by technocrats and bureaucrats who desired routine rather than change, planning rather than unpredictability. Similar ideas lay behind claims by other writers that a new 'post-capitalist' social order was emerging in which the exploitation of labour and the competitive scramble for markets were being regulated and replaced by a new breed of public and private sector managers. Such arguments have often been exaggerated, but they should not be entirely dismissed. Capitalism has changed dramatically in the last fifty years, and it is today much more difficult than it once was to identify a distinctive capitalist class.

90

At the same time, many more of us are today locked into the capitalist property system than was the case before the war. When the Wall Street stock market crashed and the rest of the financial world followed it down in 1929, only a small proportion of the population was directly affected. People lost their jobs, of course, but most workers did not have savings tied up in the financial markets. When the stock market crashed in the autumn of 1987, by contrast, millions of us were directly affected, for our future pensions, mortgage redemptions and savings were immediately put at risk. Where is the capitalist class today? It has fragmented into millions of tiny pieces. To see these pieces, look around you.

Activity

For one day, keep a diary and note down the agency which supplies you with each of the items or services you consume – the food, the TV programmes, the sociology classes, the ballpoint pen, the water from the tap. When you have completed your list, group these agencies into three categories – public sector bodies, private sector firms which are owned by particular individuals or families, and private sector firms owned by shareholders and run by managers and directors. Now try to think how these same services were provided in the mid-nineteenth century (assuming they were available). How has capitalism changed over this time? Which people today seem to have the greatest influence over your everyday life – individual capitalists, state employees or private sector managers?

The middle class

It may be difficult to identify a distinct capitalist class in modern Britain, but there is no such problem in finding the middle class. The middle class (or perhaps more accurately, the middle *classes*) has mushroomed during the twentieth century in all advanced capitalist countries, and Britain is no exception. Figures based on the 1981 census indicate that 26 per cent of the working population in Great Britain is accounted for by professional and managerial occupations. This group represents the core of the middle class today, and if we add to it other groups, such as small business people, who may also be thought to constitute part of the middle class, we end up with a figure of something over 30 per cent. However, the growth of the middle class has come almost entirely as a result of the expansion of professional, managerial and administrative occupations.

The traditional 'petty bourgeoisie'

We saw earlier in this chapter that Max Weber's approach to social stratification enabled him to distinguish two main groupings within the middle class. One, the *petty bourgeoisie*, consisted of people who made their living through ownership of property but lacked any high level managerial or professional training and qualifications. The people he had in mind were those who owned and ran small businesses – the owner of a small factory or workshop employing a handful of people, the small retailer running a newsagent's or grocery store, the self-employed plumber or builder, the landlord who owns three or four houses and lives off the rent from the tenants, the small family farmer, and so on. In Goldthorpe's schema, most of these people are treated as one of the 'intermediate classes' between the middle and working classes, but more conventional usage suggests that the petty bourgeoisie is better understood, following Weber, as one element within the middle class.

Marx expected the petty bourgeoisie to disappear as competition resulted in small firms being driven out of business. Clearly this has not happened. It is true that the relative size of the small entrepreneurial class in Britain has declined since the nineteenth century, and that the economy has increasingly come to be dominated by a relatively small number of large companies. However, it is worth remembering that the great majority of businesses today are still small businesses. In terms of their share of total turnover in the economy, their significance has certainly been declining, but the petty bourgeoisie has proved a tenacious class. In Britain, it has had to survive in a generally hostile climate of take-overs, nationalisation, increasing bureaucracy (such as the unpaid labour which businesses have to perform for the government in collecting VAT) and tight legal controls (such as rent controls on private housing), and these and other factors have meant that the rate of turnover in membership of the petty bourgeoisie has been high. Small businesses are vulnerable in the modern world, and many go bust each year, yet new firms have been founded to replace them. For many people, the possibility of 'working for yourself' continues to be alluring, even when the odds seem stacked against them.

The 'service class'

The other section of the middle class identified by Weber was the 'intelligentsia and specialists' or what various commentators have subsequently come to call the *service class*. For Weber, this stratum comprised people like civil servants, technicians and various professional groups who could command high incomes by virtue of their training and qualifications. It is this part of the middle class which has grown enormously over the years.

Education and qualifications by themselves do not, of course, guarantee high earnings. Educated and highly trained labour has been in increasing demand as technical change and the growth of administration have resulted in ever-expanding needs for specialists of various kinds. Indeed, sociologists like Daniel Bell and Alain Tourraine have gone so far as to suggest that we are moving into a 'post-industrial' era in which manufacturing is being eclipsed by the growth of services and the core economic requirements are shifting from the need for manual labour to a new emphasis on skills demanding high

93

levels of education and knowledge. Whether or not such futuristic analyses are correct, it is clear that the educated middle class finds that its labour is generally in high demand, and most members of this class enjoy secure careers and relatively high earnings.

Rewards in the labour market, of course, are a function of supply as well as demand, and Weber recognised that this section of the middle class often attempts to maintain or bolster its market value by restricting entry to others, thereby ensuring its own continued scarcity. In pursuing such strategies of 'social closure', it has often sought to enlist the help of the state – for example, through state licensing of the right to practise as in the case of medicine. Indeed, for many members of this class, the state has become the major source of new employment opportunities as it has extended its activities in areas like health, education and social welfare. Six and a half million people (27 per cent of the total workforce) were employed by the state in Britain in 1986 (5.3 million directly and a further 1.2 million in public corporations such as the nationalised industries). Many of these people are members of the 'service class'. There are nearly two million professionals employed in education, health and welfare in Britain, for example, and the vast majority of these are employed in the public sector. In Weber's day, most professional people operated in the private sector – as lawyers, doctors, accountants, etc. There has been a major change, therefore, in the employment market for professional groups.

Weber saw that this class was growing, and its expansion has continued apace since he wrote. This is partly because of the growth of a distinct management stratum in capitalist firms. As we saw in the previous section, the division of ownership and control in large capitalist enterprises has given rise to a stratum of people who run firms but do not own them. In addition, firms today employ a large number of technical specialists – financial advisers, research and development specialists, computer experts, and so on. At the very top, these sorts of people can earn spectacular salaries, and it is this group of often young and talented individuals which has received much media attention in recent years, giving rise to a new word in the English language – 'yuppies'. Such people often live in London and the south-east where they work for financial institutions in the City, or in the head offices and research and development centres of the new technology industries which have located in areas such as the M4 corridor or the area around Cambridge.

The growth of this class has been most spectacular, however, in the public sector. Here it is more geographically dispersed, for state activities are located right across the country, in schools and colleges, hospitals, local government, and so on. Particularly during the 1960s and 1970s, state expenditure on social provisions rose dramatically, and this opened up new employment opportunities, not only for professionals like teachers and social workers who were involved in providing these services, but also for administrators to organise them. In the twenty years from 1961, employment in the public sector rose by 22 per cent while that in the private sector fell by 8 per cent.

In the late sixties and early seventies, many public services were reorganised, and administrative posts expanded as a result. In the health service, the social services and local government, new patterns of organisation brought more spending and more jobs for professionals and managers alike. Local government employment rose by 70 per cent between 1961 and 1975 (the year following reorganisation). In the same years, employment in education rose by 85 per cent and that in public administration by 26 per cent. These phenomenal increases were not matched by increased quality or quantity of services, however. Staff–pupil ratios only improved by 10 per cent during the 1960s, and the availability of hospital beds per head of the population fell by 11 per cent at a time when health service employment was rising rapidly. It is difficult to escape the conclusion that the dramatic increase in spending on the welfare state in this period did a lot more to improve the wages and career prospects of

95

thousands of housing managers, health service bureaucrats and college lecturers than it did to improve the life chances of ordinary users of these services.

The division between public and private sectors within the middle class is significant, for members of each group very often share different values and certainly have different interests insofar as those working in the state sector have a vested interest in maintaining and increasing public spending, even at the expense of higher taxes levied on the private sector. Indeed, a body of literature known as 'public choice theory' has developed in recent decades which analyses the way in which those working in the state sector are able to improve their economic situation by expanding the scope of government services, thereby enhancing their own career prospects. In addition, recent work by Patrick Dunleavy and other political scientists has shown that sectoral employment is an important influence on voting behaviour. It is no longer true that the middle class as a whole votes overwhelmingly for the Conservative Party, for those employed in the public sector nowadays often vote Labour in recognition of that party's greater commitment to maintaining and increasing expenditure on state services. Indeed, while membership of trade unions generally has been falling in the 1980s, union membership among some sections of the public sector middle class has been rising, and unions like the National Union of Teachers and the National Association of Local Government Officers now represent a significant power bloc within the TUC.

Despite these significant differences, however, professionals and managers within both the public and private sectors do share much in common in terms of their work, market and status situations. In their discussion of the 'service class', Scott Lash and John Urry (1987) list various criteria which members of this class share in common. According to them, the distinctiveness of the service class lies in the fact that it occupies a dominant position in the division of labour but does not own capital. Entry into the service class is on the basis of education and formal qualifications. Members of this class enjoy a privileged work and market situation, with high levels of authority, high material rewards and relatively secure careers. In return, it is their task to 'service' the requirements of a modern capitalist society by making the capitalist system run efficiently and rationally. This means, in the private sector, planning and organising production and employing and regulating workers, while in the public sector it means organising all the services and provisions which are required to educate, house and otherwise maintain an effective labour force.

Lash and Urry point out that, in comparison with the USA, the service class in Britain developed very late. In the USA, companies in the early years of this century were strongly influenced by ideas of 'scientific management', and as a result of this they developed complex management hierarchies which resulted in an explosion of new, white-collar jobs. This in turn stimulated an expansion of educational and state bureaucracies such that a new class of educated and trained experts swiftly emerged in the middle ground between capital and labour.

In Britain, by contrast, scientific management never took off, for most British firms distrusted such new ideas and remained wedded to a more traditional ethic of amateurism. It was not until the Wilson years of the 1960s that any serious attempt was made in Britain to modernise the economy and to rationalise existing institutions, and the major thrust in this direction came from government itself. Unlike in the USA, therefore, the emphasis on education and training came very late, and it took the form of a major expansion of public sector employment. Since 1979, of course, Conservative governments have attempted to reverse the trend to increasing state management of the economy and society, but it remains the case that the emergence of the British service class from the 1960s onwards has relied to a great extent on public sector employment. More than any other single class in Britain, the service class is very much a product of the interventionist state.

The lower middle class

The feminisation of clerical work

The lower middle class is here taken to refer to people in routine clerical and service occupations, as well as those in low-level technical jobs and individuals such as foremen whose work entails some supervision of manual workers. The biggest single grouping in this class is that of routine non-manual employees in clerical, secretarial and similar occupations. In 1851, clerical workers accounted for less than 1 per cent of the employed population, and just one-tenth of 1 per cent of them were women. By 1981, clerical and related occupations had expanded to account for 16 per cent of the working population, and by then, this group was 74 per cent female. Indeed, 30 per cent of all women recorded as 'economically active' at the 1981 census were clerical workers, yet this occupational category accounted for less than 7 per cent of male workers. Not only has clerical work expanded enormously during the twentieth century, but it has become overwhelmingly a female occupation.

It follows from this that any analysis of this *social class* in British society must remain alert to the significance of gender divisions within it. It has been a major failing of much of the research on clerical and related occupations that it has focused exclusively on the work, market and status situation of men, yet we know that the labour market as a whole is remarkably segregated by gender, and there is good reason to believe that gender divisions may be just as significant within occupational groups as they are between them. Certainly it seems strange to draw conclusions on the class position of clerks, three-quarters of whom are female, on the basis of studies which look only at men.

The expansion in numbers of clerical workers, and the feminisation of the workforce, have over the years gone hand in hand with a marked decline in the status and conditions of clerks in Britain. In the nineteenth century, clerks were highly esteemed and relatively well paid men who were responsible for what was in effect a range of management functions. Today, however, the status of this sort of work has declined, and wages, security and responsibility have declined with it. What we are dealing with here is an occupational category whose economic and social position in the division of labour has changed completely. The nineteenth-century clerk is probably better seen as an early forerunner of today's service class (in which men still outnumber women by around two to one) than a predecessor of today's clerical workers. When we look at clerical workers today, we are looking at a stratum which has undergone quite dramatic downward block mobility.

The proletarianisation of clerical workers?

Earlier in this chapter, we briefly considered David Lockwood's pioneering study, *The Blackcoated Worker*. Researched and written in the 1950s, this study showed that, although the status situation of routine non-manual workers had declined, the advantages they enjoyed in their work and market situations were still such as to mark them off from the manual working class. The question is whether this is still true thirty years on.

In his influential study, *Labor and Monopoly Capital*, Harry Braverman (1974) argued forcibly that clerical workers (and, indeed, personal service workers) have become part of the working class of modern capitalism: 'In its conditions of employment, this working population has lost all former superiorities over workers in industry, and in its scales of pay it has sunk almost to the very bottom' (Braverman: 355). Drawing mainly on American evidence, he argued that clerical incomes are now on average lower than those of manual workers, and that to all intents and purposes, clerical labour is no different from manual labour on the factory floor. The close personal contact between clerks and their employers has been broken: clerical work has been subdivided

99

into a range of monotonous single functions such as keyboard operating, filing and work on the switchboard; and the modern office has been mechanised and computerised to such an extent that most clerical functions now involve no more mental activity than is required on a factory production line. Clerks, secretaries and the like have, in Braverman's view, been 'proletarianised', and one indication of this is their increasing participation in characteristically working-class movements such as trade unions.

There is some truth in what Braverman argues, for office work has been transformed by technology (particularly the introduction of computers) to a point where the division between manual labour on the shopfloor and mental labour in the office now makes much less sense than it once did. In their study of clerical work in three different bureaucratic organisations (a bank, a life assurance company and a local authority), Crompton and Jones (1984) showed that many clerical tasks have now been 'deskilled' by the introduction of electronic data processing which has the effect of breaking down processes into simple stages and centralising control at the top of the office hierarchy. In their study, 89 per cent of the clerks interviewed performed tasks involving computers – some prepared input, others worked with VDUs, others dealt with output. Furthermore, 91 per cent were found to exercise no control or discretion over their work and most of these people needed only to be able to read, write and follow simple instructions in order to perform the tasks required of them.

This study also confirmed Braverman's argument that clerical wages have fallen relative to manual workers' wages. As late as 1936, male clerks were earning the same average wages as skilled manual workers. Since then they have fallen behind, so much so that in 1978, the average earnings of semiskilled male manual workers overtook the average earnings of male clerks for the first time.

Nevertheless, we should remain sceptical of the proletarianisation thesis. In their study, Marshall and his colleagues found no evidence to support Braverman's claims among their white-collar respondents. They argue that the work tasks of clerical employees have not been deskilled and that they still enjoy much greater job autonomy than manual workers do. Furthermore, they are much more likely to think of themselves as 'middle class' than are manual workers. These authors recognise that some sales workers may be virtually indistinguishable now from the working class, but they insist that most members of this intermediate stratum in British society are neither objectively nor subjectively proletarian (see Marshall *et al.* 1988: Chapter 5).

Crompton and Jones too are critical of Braverman's thesis. This is because technical deskilling does not necessarily mean that the social definition of a task changes. Some clerical labour is still defined as skilled even though it requires little technical competence to perform it. Most employers have retained or even extended detailed grading differentials even where automation has reduced the gap in skill levels between different positions. Furthermore, as the competence required in clerical labour has declined, so the formal qualifications required at entry, and later for promotion, have increased! It may be that most clerical work demands little more than an ability to read and write, but most employers of clerical labour now insist on four GCSE Grade 3 passes as a minimum entry requirement. Technical deskilling has not therefore eroded differentiation based on notional skills and responsibilities. As clerks acquire more years of service and more post-entry qualifications, so they move up a hierarchy to positions which may be little different from those below them in terms of complexity of the work, but which are more highly rewarded in terms of income and status. The problem, however, is that it is more often men than women who make such moves upwards.

The higher up the ladder we move, the greater the proportion of men occupying these positions. Twenty-one out of 157 women in Crompton and Jones's sample were promoted, compared with 53 out of 101 men. Other studies of clerks have argued that a major distinction between clerical and manual work concerns the possibilities of promotion within and beyond clerical grades. However, it is Crompton and Jones's contention that such possibilities are virtually monopolised by males. Promotion, and the upward social mobility which may go with it, is in their view nowhere near as common as has generally been imagined. A majority of male clerks can realistically expect to advance in their careers, but this is only possible because so many female clerks stay where they are.

Activity

If you are a member of an organisation such as a school or college, get hold of a list of staff names. This may be in the form of an internal telephone directory, an organisation chart or whatever. Distinguish between higher level administrative offices and more routine clerical and secretarial functions. What is the proportion of men to women in each category? If your list indicates the marital status of women, see how many are single and how many are married. Now relate your data to the arguments developed by Crompton and Jones. Do your data support their arguments?

Gender and class among clerical workers

The clerical stratum has been fractured along the lines of gender. Women are concentrated in the lower grades, and although their poor promotion prospects may sometimes be explained in terms of employer discrimination, the main reason for it is that the career ladder has been constructed in such a way that most women cannot hope to climb up it. Most men in Crompton and Jones's sample of clerical workers could expect some sort of promotion by the time they were thirty-five. It is this sense of routine clerical work as a springboard into higher positions which has been cited by many critics of Braverman as evidence against the proletarianisation thesis. Crompton and Jones, however, believe that much of this movement takes place across a relatively short range in that even higher positions generally involve few effective managerial functions. Furthermore, the extent of such movement has been exaggerated by neglecting the issue of the great majority of women who stay put.

According to these authors, the clerical career structure mitigates against women because they cannot meet the criteria of merit which most (male-dominated) managements lay down. Although younger women are often just as committed to building a career as their male counterparts, they are massively inhibited by their later domestic commitments. Breaks for childbirth, problems in moving to a different area of the country in pursuit of career advancement, and a failure to acquire post-entry qualifications all work against female career development. The result is that men move onwards and upwards into jobs which are defined as more skilled and responsible while women tend to remain in lower grades which are held in low esteem and are generally poorly rewarded. It follows from this analysis that men build their careers only because women do not. Given that most clerks are female, any future increase in women's commitments to developing a career would have a dramatic impact on the favoured prospects currently enjoyed by men, and Crompton and Jones speculate that this may now be happening. If they are right, then the traditional career prospects enjoyed by men are likely to suffer as more women come to compete for the limited opportunities which are available.

What, then, of David Lockwood's argument thirty years ago that the work and market situations of clerks are sufficient to distinguish them from the working class? If we focus on *male* clerical workers, this would appear to be true, since for many of them, a clerical job is the first rung on a ladder leading to positions which are still quite distinct from those of most manual workers. This does not make them middle class, but it does differentiate them from the working class. Typically, they can expect greater job security: in 1981, the unemployment rate among routine non-manual workers was 4 per cent as compared with 8 per cent for skilled manual workers and 13 per cent for unskilled manual workers. They can also expect their earnings to continue rising through their working lives while manual worker earnings tend to peak in early middle age, after which they drop on average by between 10 and 20 per cent by the time of retirement. Furthermore, when they get to retirement, clerical workers are far more likely to enjoy the benefits of a private pension scheme. Hours of work for the two groups also differ quite markedly – the 1988 edition of *Social Trends* shows that male manual workers work on average 44.5 hours per week (made up of 39 hours basic plus 5½ hours overtime) compared with an average of 38.6 hours worked by male white collar employees.

Female clerical workers in lower grades also share some of these advantages, of course. As Marshall and his co-authors rightly emphasise, they generally enjoy with their male colleagues greater job security and shorter hours than most manual workers. But because they are concentrated in the lower grades, it is women who have generally experienced the most deleterious effects of workplace mechanisation, and their career blockage means that their lifetime prospects in terms of income and responsibility are much less rosy. Just as the middle class is divided, so too is the lower middle class, only here the key division is that based on gender. Sociological studies of clerical work which have focused solely on men have been right to insist on the real division between their situation and that of manual workers. When we include female workers, however, the division becomes less vivid, and the boundary marking off one class from another seems rather more arbitrary.

The working class

The OPCS divides the manual working class into three categories – skilled workers such as fitters, bus drivers and trained coalface workers; semi-skilled workers like machinists, bus conductors and storekeepers; and unskilled workers such as labourers, refuse collectors and cleaners. The manual working class as a whole has been shrinking and by the 1981 census accounted for just 51 per cent of the employed population. This shrinkage has been particularly marked in the unskilled stratum as technological change has reduced demand for sheer muscle power: unskilled manual workers make up less than 7 per cent of the workforce. This compares with the skilled workers who still represent one quarter of all those employed (and 36 per cent of all the men employed) in Britain.

The growth of working-class affluence

Not only has the size of the working class been reducing, but the nature of this class seems to have been changing. This is often reflected in popular imagery such as the much-repeated observation that the 'cloth cap' is disappearing. At his party's annual conference in 1987, the Labour Party leader, Neil Kinnock, made reference to changes in the working class when he commented on the need to represent, not just the poor, but also the docker who earns £300 a week and owns a villa in Marbella. What lies behind observations like this is the sense that, although the working class is still at or near the bottom of the earnings and status hierarchy, a general rise in affluence has changed its style of life just as much as it has affected higher class groups.

That living standards have been rising for all classes is undeniable. *Social Trends* shows that total disposable incomes in 1986 were 30 per cent higher in real terms (that is, allowing for inflation) than they were ten years earlier. On average, household spending power rose by 2.5 per cent every year during this period, yet this was a time when the economy went into its worst slump since the 1930s. This increased standard of living is reflected in the growth of ownership of housing and consumer goods across all classes. We saw earlier in the chapter, for example, that home ownership has been rising in the working class to a point where 64 per cent of skilled workers, 46 per cent of semi-skilled workers and 33 per cent of unskilled workers now own their homes. Two-thirds of households have a car today compared with only one-third in 1961. Eighty-six per cent of British homes now own a colour television set, 80 per cent have a telephone, 28 per cent have a video. Thirty-three million people out of a population of fifty-six and a half million took holidays in Britain in 1985 and a further sixteen million went abroad. Nineteen per cent of adults owned shares in 1987 including one in six skilled manual workers and one in twelve semi- and unskilled workers. All this and more represents striking evidence for Hayek's 'moving column' thesis, for income differentials between the classes may not have changed all that much, but every class is a lot better off than it was even one generation ago. The one exception, of course, concerns the unemployed whose numbers have more than tripled since the early 1970s. We shall consider their situation later.

In strict sociological terms, the fact that the working class has become more affluent and now owns a range of goods which was out of its reach just a short time ago does nothing to alter its class situation. As we have seen, social class has to do with how people get their incomes, not how they spend them. Nevertheless, rising affluence is likely to influence working-class culture and ways of life. Taken together with the extensive opportunities for upward social mobility which we analysed earlier, it does not seem unreasonable to suppose that increased affluence may have influenced the way in which working-class people see their society and their own place within it.

Variations in working-class images of society

Rising affluence is not a new phenomenon. Incomes and living standards rose continuously through the twenty years following the Second World War, and by the late 1950s, many observers were already suggesting that this was reshaping the traditional character of the working class. Such arguments seemed to receive support from electoral patterns at that time, for the Conservative Party won three successive general election victories through the 1950s and it was obvious that this could not have happened without substantial working-class support. Pundits began to speculate that the working class was changing and that the Labour Party would never again win power unless it too changed and began to appeal to the mass of comfortable and affluent Britons.

To many observers, affluence was breaking down old class divisions and reordering traditional political allegiances. Some suggested that capitalism itself was being transcended as the welfare state, Keynesian full employment policies and the bi-partisan commitment to the 'mixed economy' were producing a new, post-capitalist era. In this view, old class cleavages were becoming blurred and a new kind of 'mass society' was developing in which everybody was a consumer of universal state services, generalised mass media, and widely available consumer goods. In this changed context, the working class was coming more and more to live like the middle class, think like the middle class and vote like the middle class. Hire purchase, full employment, new technology and welfare state orange juice had together worked the magic of making the working class increasingly indistinguishable from the middle class. Britain was becoming a middle-class society and workers were undergoing a process of *embourgeoisement*.

Such arguments always were grossly overgeneralised. As we have seen repeatedly through this book, social stratification is about more than simply income. In addition to people's market situation, we have also to consider their work and status situations. Thus, in a celebrated article published in 1966, David Lockwood argued that social changes were affecting different sections of the working class in different ways. Focusing on people's work and market situations, as well as their social standing and patterns of interaction within their local communities, Lockwood identified three distinct types of manual worker, each of which was likely to view the world in very different ways.

The first of these he termed *traditional proletarians*. Drawing upon various sociological studies of work and social life among groups like coal miners, dockers and shipbuilders, he showed that the work situation for this group tended to encourage strong attachments to workmates and a powerful sense of class solidarism. Workers in these occupations may work in gangs or small and cohesive groups in which they come to know and rely upon each other, and they rarely catch sight of managers or owners of the enterprise. They are strongly unionised, and the emotional bonds of fraternalism which are nurtured at work are often carried over into life outside where whole communities are often grouped around a single source of employment such as the village pit, the shipyard, the docks, or whatever. Men in these communities tend to spend their leisure time in pubs and clubs drinking with their workmates, while their wives and daughters lead strikingly separate lives based on the home. The experience of daily life in such working-class communities generates and sustains a dichotomous view of society in terms of a clear class division between 'us' (the workers) and 'them' (the bosses).

Traditional deferential workers, by contrast, are to be found mainly in small towns and rural areas and are often employed in service industries, agriculture and family firms. They know their employer personally and their social standing is determined more by face-to-face interaction within tight-knit communities than by membership of any nationally recognised class stratum. Their work and community situation encourages vertical rather than horizontal identification, and their view of the world is one in which different people are finely graded along a status hierarchy. They recognise the right to rule of traditional leaders, such as the country squire, and they are sceptical of new wealth. A perfect example of such an individual is Scullion, the college porter in Tom Sharpe's novel, *Porterhouse Blue*. A guardian of crusty college traditions and an admirer of the young upper-class gentlemen who pass through the university, Scullion endorses the paternal authority of decrepit scholars while sullenly resenting the changes introduced by a new Master who is committed to values of meritocracy and modernism.

The third group identified by Lockwood was the *privatised workers*. These people work in relatively modern industries such as engineering, chemicals and car assembly. They also tend to live on new and largely anonymous housing estates away from the places and people with whom they grew up, and enjoying few contacts with their neighbours. Their work situation encourages identification with neither workmates nor employers, for the repetitive and alienative work tasks lead them to focus on their life outside of work as their major interest and source of identity. Work for them is simply a means of earning money so that they can pay for the mortgage, the family holiday and the consumer durables which are the features of their private lives. They have no sense of belonging to a particular class or social status group, but rather see themselves as members of a broad mass of income earners in which people are distinguished from one another only in terms of marginal differences in the amount of money they earn. Such workers will often join trade unions, but they do so simply to safeguard and enhance their earnings, for they share no sense of emotional fraternalism.

It was, of course, this third group which commentators had in mind when they claimed that the working class was becoming middle-class. Traditional proletarians like coal miners, and traditional deferentialists like farm workers, were clearly leading lives which in no sense led them to share the experiences and values of classes higher up the income and status ladder. The privatised workers, on the other hand, did look like a new and different stratum, for their relatively high incomes enabled them to participate in ways of life more often associated with middle-class people, and their values were quite distinct from those of the miners' lodge or the village hall. Were they, then, the vanguard of a growing process of embourgeoisement?

A process of embourgeoisement?

In the mid-1960s, David Lockwood and three colleagues then at Cambridge University – John Goldthorpe, Frank Bechhofer and Jennifer Platt – set out to test this hypothesis through a study of workers employed in the car and chemical industries in Luton. Their three volumes of findings, which became known collectively as the 'Affluent Worker' study, have become a classic of British empirical sociology.

They tested the embourgeoisement thesis by considering three questions. The first concerned the experience at work, and here they showed that high incomes and new work processes brought about as a result of technological and management changes had not in themselves altered the objective position of these workers. Rather, work was often experienced negatively. Rates of job satisfaction were low, overtime and shift working were normal and there was little interest in or commitment to enhancing or enriching the work experience. They did not identify with the firm and were not interested in out-of-hours works social activities, they were not bothered by the lack of promotion opportunities and did not seek more responsibility, they were not concerned about divisions (such as separate canteen facilities) between themselves and the white collar employees. Rather, these workers shared what the authors termed an 'instrumental' attitude to their employment – it was a means to an end – and in most cases this reflected a prior orientation on their part. In other words, many of these workers chose to work on assembly lines or in other routine and monotonous jobs precisely because they were willing to trade off job satisfaction against high earnings. In all of this, they differed markedly from the white-collar grades. The authors concluded, 'So far at least as the world of work is concerned, the thesis of working-class embourgeoisement can have little relevance to present day British society' (1969: 83).

Much the same conclusion arose in response to their second question which concerned patterns of sociability outside of work. Here the authors agreed that standards of domestic living enjoyed by these workers were no different from those characteristic of white collar employees. However, they showed that their styles of life were different, for the manual workers did not socialise much with people from work, husband and wife often developed different friendships rather than socialising as a couple, home entertaining was rare, and membership of formal voluntary associations was very low. Much of this could be explained by the experience of work itself, for the drudgery at work led these workers to seek compensation through privatised, home-based leisure pursuits in which they relied for social contact on their immediate family rather than on friends. Furthermore, such friends as they had were usually other manual workers – they were not interacting with middle-class people, and this continued class segregation outside work was seen by the authors as another crucial factor in refuting the embourgeoisement thesis.

Finally, the study considered the aspirations and views of the world shared by these workers. Here it was found that they were strongly consumerist in their orientations – their aims were generally to purchase this or that item rather than to rise up the status pecking order. They had hopes for their children's advancement, but unlike the middle class, did not have the cultural capital to invest in order to bring these hopes to realistic fruition. Their view of the social world did not recognise the subtle status distinctions by which the middle classes differentiate themselves and others, but rather focused on money. In this way, they saw themselves as members of one large income class incorporating virtually the whole of British society apart from the very rich and the very poor.

On all three criteria, then, the embourgeoisement thesis was rejected. It had been tested on the group of workers to whom it was most likely to apply, and had been found invalid. The

111

authors accepted that affluence *has* changed the material conditions of working class people, and that this *does* have important consequences (for example, in changing the basis of commitment to trade unionism), but they denied that these changes support any claim that the working class is therefore disappearing.

A new 'middle mass'?

The 'Affluent Worker' study effectively killed off academic concern with the issue of embourgeoisement for nearly twenty years. Recently, however, the thesis has re-emerged, though in rather different form. As in the 1950s, so too in the 1980s, working-class living standards have been rising and a sustained consumer spending boom has meant that many working-class people have bought their houses, filled them with various goods and gadgets and made them into the principal focus of their lives. The old staple industries like coal and shipbuilding have been run down over these years while new technologies have generated new kinds of working-class employment and have transformed the work process in industries like printing and electronics. On top of all this, the Conservative Party has secured three successive general election victories since 1979 just as it did in the years from 1951 to 1959.

All of this has led some sociologists to ask whether the embourgeoisement thesis was perhaps developed a quarter of a century in advance of its time. If the workers of the sixties were not shedding their class skin, what of the workers of the eighties and nineties?

One of the most important studies of recent years – Ray Pahl's (1984) *Divisions of Labour* – showed that working-class households in the Isle of Sheppey in Kent enjoyed a comfortable and home-centred style of life where two or more members of the household were able to contribute money from earnings. There was, he found, a major division within the working class between 'work-rich' and 'work-poor' households. The former enjoy relatively high household incomes, tend to own their own homes and engage in various forms of self-provisioning such as gardening and DIY. The latter subsist on low incomes, lack the resources to fend for themselves and depend increasingly upon the state for their housing and sustenance. In a later paper, Pahl (1988) suggests that this division between core and peripheral households is becoming more marked and that it is resulting in a reshaping of class cleavages as work-rich households merge into the relatively comfortable 'middle mass' while work-poor households become increasingly impoverished and marginalised.

Some Marxists have also begun to take seriously the possibility that the working class as it developed in the early period of capitalism may now be disappearing. Andre Gorz, in a book entitled *Farewell to the Working Class*, suggests that technological developments are now removing the need for much manual labour and that paid employment is no longer the central life activity for many people. Socialism, he claims, is 'historically obsolete' in advanced industrial societies (Gorz 1982: 12), for most workers today do not feel any sense of belonging to the working class, or indeed to any other class, and they are not interested in collectivistic political strategies or the prospect of a socially planned economy. Workers no longer seek to free themselves within work, but now look to free themselves from work. The central part of most people's lives today is not their employment but the private realm of family, home and garden – 'a private niche protecting one's personal life against all pressures and external social obligations . . . Real life begins outside of work, and work itself has become a means towards the extension of the sphere of non-work' (Gorz 1982: 80–1).

All of this is highly reminiscent of the debate over affluence thirty years ago, for here too we find references to the marginality of work in people's lives, the importance of the private sphere, the failure to identify with any social class and the idea that the working class is disappearing. If even Marxist theorists are now saying these things, the time has

113

surely come to re-open the files on the changing nature of the working class.

As in the sixties, so too today it is important not to generalise too far. As the Crompton and Jones study of clerical workers shows, new technology may 'proletarianise' workers just as much as it 'embourgeoisifies' them. While it is true that new jobs have been created as a result of revolutions in micro-electronics, these often turn out to be routine, poorly paid and predominantly female. Although the working class, and particularly the unskilled working class, is getting ever smaller, it seems premature to bid it farewell as Gorz seeks to do.

Nevertheless, the sorts of changes outlined at the start of this section – factors like the growth of real earnings and the spread of home ownership – are clearly important and they may be leaving their mark on working-class culture. Various studies of the significance of home ownership, for example, have suggested that it reflects and contributes to values of individualism and privatism which would seem to run counter to more traditional conceptions of working-class collectivism. But the evidence here is still scanty and interpretations of it are diverse. The study of the British class system conducted by researchers at the University of Essex has suggested, for example, that there is nothing new in working-class privatism and that it is in any case not necessarily inconsistent with continued support for and participation in collectivist organisations such as trade unions and the Labour Party. They suggest that in the nineteenth century home-centred privatised life styles co-existed with high levels of participation in collectivist organisations such as Working Men's clubs and trade unions, and that the same is true today. Like Goldthorpe and Lockwood before them, these authors thus emphasise the continuity rather than the change in working-class social and political life, and they firmly reject any suggestion that class identities may be weakening.

Activities

1 Photocopy a street map of the town nearest to where you live. Now look up in *Yellow Pages* the addresses of all the video shops and plot them on the map. Do they cluster in any particular kinds of areas or are they spread through both working-class and middle-class neighbourhoods? Try standing in your local video hire shop one evening for half an hour or so. What kinds of people seem to be hiring videos – are they mainly working-class, middle-class or a mixture of both?

   Note: Britain has the highest rate of video ownership in the world and some observers believe this is an indicator of a high level of privatism and home-centredness in our lives. Watching a video means we need not venture out to the cinema, which is a more collective experience. Can you think of any other examples of goods or services which we now consume in our private homes but which used to be more communal?

2 Various official statistical sources are available which provide data on ownership of consumer durables. Try *Social Trends*, the *Family Expenditure Survey* and the *General Household Survey* (if the college library does not have them, the reference library should). How do patterns of ownership break down across different social classes? Do you think it makes any difference to how people think of their social class identities if they buy a house, or a car or a new kitchen?

Conservatism and the working class

The Essex research team has also cast some doubt on the view, expressed by many writers, that the class basis of voting is breaking down and that the working class is becoming detached from socialism. In the 1980s, Labour has performed spectacularly badly in electoral terms. In 1983 it won its lowest percentage of the vote (27.6 per cent) since 1918 when it only contested two-thirds of the seats, and its recovery in 1987 (when it raised its vote by just 3 per cent) was marginal. In 1983, Labour won only 5 per cent more manual worker votes than the Conservatives did, and only 38 per cent of manual workers supported the party as compared with 62 per cent in 1959 when the Conservatives last won a similar landslide victory. The biggest single desertion from Labour occurred among manual worker home owners, and of those who had bought their council houses, 56 per cent voted Conservative and only 18 per cent Labour.

Figures like these have sustained a so-called 'class dealignment thesis' in which it is argued that the working class has become detached from Labourism, either because more people now vote on the issues rather than by habit, or because factors other than class (such as housing tenure and sectoral employment) are coming to play a more significant role in shaping political alignments. It would seem to follow from this that the working class is indeed changing as the general level of affluence and private ownership of housing and consumer goods rises. Patrick Dunleavy (1979), for example, suggests on the basis of evidence from the 1974 elections that the combined effect of home ownership and car ownership now outweighs the importance of occupational class, and in this he is supported to some extent by research in Manchester by Vic Duke and Stephen Edgell (1984) who found that support for Labour and for policies of state provision depends not simply on social class, but additionally on whether workers own their homes, own cars, have private health insurance, and so on. If this is the case, then we may expect working-class support for capitalism, and for unambiguously capitalist parties, to rise as access to private forms of consumption rises.

Such arguments are, however, contested by the Essex research team. On the basis of their 1984 survey data, they admit that the working class (defined in terms of Goldthorpe's

116

schema) has divided politically – half of the skilled manual workers they interviewed did not support Labour – and that factors like home ownership do seem to be associated with political alignments (Marshall *et al.* 1988). However, they do not accept that this indicates any growth in working-class antipathy to socialism. They point out that Labour Party support has fallen in all classes which could indicate simply that the Party is going through a bad patch rather than that it is losing its traditional support base. They also point out that the core working class is still quite strongly Labour. While one-third of working-class people vote Conservative, this figure drops to one-fifth among those who were themselves born into this class. Furthermore, Labour voting is strong among those who identify themselves as working-class. They conclude from all this that class is still the key to political sympathies and values in Britain and that the core working class has been deserting Labour, not because it no longer feels it is working-class, but because Labour has been expressing inadequately its class values and interests. It is not, therefore, the working class which has changed, but the Labour Party!

The current uncertain state of knowledge about the working class in Britain makes it difficult to come to any definite conclusions as to the significance of recent changes, and it would certainly be foolhardy to try to predict future developments. All that we can say with any certainty is that the working class has been getting smaller, that this seems likely to continue, and that most members of this class have been growing more affluent. That the working class is changing therefore seems undeniable. Whether these changes are producing a different kind of culture and way of life, and whether they are undermining the social basis of support for socialism in this country, are questions to which sociology does not as yet have any very firm answers.

The underclass

Class analysis and the unwaged

The majority of people in Britain are not in employment of any kind. Many are children who must stay in school until at least the age of sixteen. They presumably fall outside the scope of class analysis altogether. Even excluding the under-sixteens, however, 54 per cent of women and 22 per cent of men were classified in the 1981 census as 'economically inactive'. Retired people account for a large slice of this group in both sexes (15 per cent of all men and 8 per cent of all women are classified as retired). Students over the age of sixteen make up another 3 per cent of the adult population, and people classed as 'permanently sick' constitute a further 4 per cent. Twenty-one per cent of the total are other economically inactive people, 99 per cent of whom are women who in everyday language would be referred to as housewives.

None of these people (who together make up 39 per cent of the adult population) can easily, or perhaps even sensibly, be accommodated within conventional class analysis. Sociologists of various different persuasions have sometimes tried to include one or other of these groups within class theory. Students, permanently sick and retired people, for example, are analysed by Erik Olin Wright in terms of their 'class trajectory' (that is, the class to which they are headed or from which they have come), and married women are classified by Goldthorpe (and many others) according to the class of their husbands (even when they have a job themselves). More recently, various writers have tried to come to grips with the position of housewives in the class system and have argued either that women should be treated as a separate class (a proposal which would place a cleaner and a Prime Minister in the same category), or that a different class schema needs to be developed for women given the gender segmentation of the labour market (see, for example, Dale, Gilbert and Arber

118

1985). Although such proposals are interesting and often innovative, they rarely succeed in convincing many other sociologists. The basic problem is that, whether we follow Weber (for whom class has to do with economic power within labour and property markets) or Marx (who sees it in terms of relations to the means of production), it seems invalid to allocate people to a class situation when they have no paid occupation.

Most of our discussion in this book, therefore, has related only to the 61 per cent of the adult population which is 'economically active'. Yet even this figure includes a sizeable number of people who are unemployed! Taking them out reduces the proportion of the adult population actually participating in the formal economy to 55 per cent, and it is they who are distributed among the various social classes we have been discussing.

What, then, can we say about the rest? They are, of course, a very varied group. Some 'housewives' are extremely well off while others (often single parents) clearly live at or near the poverty line. Townsend (1979) found that 25 per cent of one-parent families (compared with just 4 per cent of two-parent families) received an income below supplementary benefit level once their housing costs were taken into account. Similarly, retirement can be associated with poverty but many retired people are relatively affluent. Townsend found that 20 per cent of pensioners have a net disposable income below this basic poverty level, but then again, 19 per cent enjoyed incomes of at least twice this figure. Even unemployment can mean different things in different households depending on factors such as whether there are other adult earners, how long the period of unemployment lasts, how much can be claimed in tax rebates and housing costs, and so on.

The idea of an underclass

In recent years, the idea has developed that *some* of these people who do not regularly participate in the formal

119

economy might validly be said to represent an 'underclass' in British society. Although Marxists tend not to use the term, the concept of an 'underclass' is not so very different from Marx's analysis of those he termed the 'reserve army of labour' or capitalism's 'surplus population' (Marx 1976: 794–8). He identified five sub-categories within this stratum: older workers who lose their jobs; workers in agriculture who are looking to move into industrial employment; a pool of irregularly employed people who take on work in a piecemeal fashion; paupers and others who cannot work; and the 'lumpenproletariat' whom Marx identified in true Victorian fashion as vagabonds, criminals and prostitutes.

According to Marx, these groups perform a vital function for capitalism in that they represent expendable labour-power. When the economy is booming, they can be drafted into the labour force in order to keep wages down; when the economy slumps, they can then be repelled out of it again. This is perhaps where the idea of an underclass diverges from the older concept of a 'reserve army', for when people talk of an underclass, they have in mind a stratum of the population which is unlikely ever to be required by the modern capitalist economy. The underclass is a permanently marginalised section of the population. It seems surplus to economic requirements, and high rates of long-term unemployment make it difficult to argue that its members are essential to the efficient functioning of a capitalist economy, for there are many who will never find work again.

The idea of the underclass or the reserve army has come to be applied to a variety of different groups in recent years. Some writers have applied it to women on the grounds that much female labour is effectively casualised. Twenty-four per cent of the economically active female population works part-time, and as we saw when we discussed clerical work, many women move in and out of the workforce as a result of marriage, childbirth or other external changes in their lives. Others, like Rex and Tomlinson (1979), have identified ethnic minority groups as a distinct underclass. Many West Indians, for example, were recruited to fill vacancies in Britain in the 1950s, and there is a parallel here with what Marx says about the way rural labour was recruited at times of expansion during the nineteenth century. As unemployment has risen in the 1980s, so it has often been these workers from the former colonies who have lost their jobs, while the younger generation of Afro-Caribbeans seems to have encountered particular problems in getting any sort of job at all after leaving school.

The peculiarities of female and ethnic minority employment experiences are clearly significant, but it obviously makes little sense to generalise to the point of arguing that women as a whole or blacks as a whole now represent the new underclass. Nor can we even claim that the unemployed *per se* are an underclass, for this is a category which is constantly shifting. At the time of writing (1989), the official unemployment rate stands at around two million, but less than one-third of these are people who have been without work for a year or more. Unemployment is certainly more characteristic of unskilled and semi-skilled workers (and of unqualified school leavers) than of other groups, but it is not peculiar to them. Every year in Britain, several million people lose or leave one job, register for a while as unemployed, and then find new employment, and they are drawn from all classes.

Having said all this, however, it is probably useful to talk of the existence of an underclass if by this we mean a stratum of people who are generally poor, unqualified and irregularly or never `employed. This underclass is disproportionately recruited today from among Afro-Caribbeans, people living in the north, those who are trapped in run-down council estates or in decaying inner cities, and young single people and single-parent families. It is an ill-defined and nebulous stratum, and because of this, it is extremely difficult to gauge its size. Dahrendorf (1987) estimates that it accounts for around 5 per cent of the population, and this seems a reasonable figure to take.

The features of the underclass

There are four key features of the underclass: it suffers multiple deprivation, it is socially marginal, it is almost entirely dependent upon state welfare provisions, and its culture is one of resigned fatalism.

As regards *multiple deprivation*, Dahrendorf writes:

> One of the characteristics of this new class is that it suffers from a culmination of social pathologies. Members of the underclass tend to have a low level of educational attainment; many have not finished school; there is much functional and even absolute illiteracy. Incomplete families are the rule rather than the exception. Housing conditions for the underclass are usually miserable; to some extent this class is an inner city phenomenon . . . It is also a phenomenon of race.

(Dahrendorf 1987: 12–13)

These various social and economic disadvantages tend to reinforce each other. The worst schools, for example, are in the inner city areas. The children of the underclass are therefore more likely to end up ill-educated and unqualified. This not only means that they find it difficult to get work, but illiteracy and ignorance also contribute to an inability to function effectively in the everyday life of a modern society. If you find it difficult filling in forms, reading instructions, expressing yourself coherently, then you are likely to keep making mistakes, missing opportunities, misunderstanding information.

This is part of the *social marginality* of the underclass, for the members of this class are effectively shut out of effective participation in mainstream society. The underclass has not by and large shared in the rising prosperity of the post-war years. It cannot aspire to own a house, or to fly off on a foreign holiday, or to drive a car. It probably lacks a telephone. Many members of this class live in marginal areas such as hard-to-let council estates or run-down inner city enclaves where crime is rife and where outsiders never care to go. Some council estates (such as the Broadwater Farm estate in Tottenham where rioting broke out in 1985) have now become so dangerous that doctors, milkmen and postal delivery workers refuse to go there. It is often impossible to get credit if you live in one of these areas. Because they are unemployed or only casually employed, members of the underclass do not belong to trade unions, and they know nothing about politics. They are unorganised and fragmented, and mainstream society comes to regard them as threatening, a problem to be policed and contained. Dahrendorf suggests that 'citizenship has become an exclusive rather than an inclusive status. Some are full citizens, some are not' (Dahrendorf 1987: 14). It is almost as if the underclass has become the outcaste of modern British society.

A factor which Dahrendorf does not discuss but which is crucial to an understanding of the underclass is that it is wholly *dependent on state welfare*. This is a client class, locked into a patronage state. The members of this class rarely contribute but always receive, rarely act but are always acted upon. They must take whatever the state deems it appropriate to hand out – a council flat with no choice of where to live; hours spent in the social security office haggling over payments which have not arrived in time to meet the bills; free school meals for the children. In such a crippling role of absolute dependency, it is impossible to sustain a positive self-image, for members of this class are never called upon to exercise judgement, make choices, achieve goals. They have been disabled by a state welfare system which claims to be helping them. As Milton and Rose Friedman argue, the welfare state has

> put some people in a position to decide what is good for other people. The effect is to instil in the one group a feeling of almost God-like power; in the other a feeling of child-like dependence. The capacity of the beneficiaries for independence, for making their own decisions, atrophies through disuse.
>
> (M. and R. Friedman 1980: 149)

123

This then, feeds the *culture of fatalism* which is so characteristic of the underclass. The young are not always fatalistic – they may rebel, develop a counter-culture, flout authority, steal what they need or even riot in the street as in some of the inner city areas in 1981 and 1985. But as they grow into adulthood and find themselves in a grubby flat with several children, no money and no way to spend their time constructively, there develops a culture of fatalism and resignation which sociologists have generally referred to as a 'culture of poverty'. In the 1960s, many sociologists came to argue against the existence of such a culture, for the idea that negative attitudes and values are reproduced from one generation to the next seemed to suggest that the poor were responsible for their own plight, and many left-wing sociologists shied away from such an offensive conclusion. To some extent they were right, for the culture of poverty is as much a product of a hopeless situation as it is a cause of it. Material deprivation breeds fatalism and despair which in turn reproduce material deprivation. Some people manage to escape this cycle, but for those who remain, hope and initiative are gradually crushed as they inexorably become resigned to their fates. For example, research done by Marie Jahoda on the unemployed in the 1930s showed how lack of a structured day results in a loss of time and work discipline, and these findings have now been repeated in studies conducted by Ian Miles and others in the 1980s. Inactivity breeds apathy. Empty hours are filled with sleep, and days go by in a dull haze of television programmes and signing on. Sooner or later, the unemployed become unemployable, and even when jobs are found they are swiftly lost.

What is to be done?

Much ink has been spilled over the years by sociologists and others discussing what can be done about this marginalised minority in British society – a minority which grows accustomed to its dependency because it is never in a position to contribute anything to society nor to participate effectively within it. Observers on the left have often suggested that nothing much can be done in the context of a capitalist society which creates a substratum of poverty as the condition of capital accumulation, and these writers have sometimes looked to the underclass itself as a potential revolutionary force and see in the inner city riots of 1981 and 1985 the initial stirrings of this insurrectionary minority. But not only is this a counsel of despair, it also seems highly unrealistic. A pervading culture of fatalism cannot easily be mobilised into a force for radical change, and when and as sporadic outbursts of unrest occur, they can in any case generally be contained by force. Precisely because this class has become detached from the mainstream of British society, it is unlikely to mobilise effectively within it.

In his discussion of policy options, Dahrendorf makes two important observations. First, he argues that the underclass will not disappear with future economic growth because it is insulated from any 'trickle-down' benefits which growth may bring. Indeed, in his view, the underclass has in a sense been created by economic growth, for manufacturing industry can now produce ever more goods using ever fewer people. Manufacturing employment in Britain fell from over eight million in 1971 to under five and a half million in 1985. Expansion of service employment (from eleven and a half million to fourteen million) made up some of the shortfall, but much of this was employment for well-educated and qualified people. As a result of the success of trade unions and wages councils in maintaining wage rates in relatively low-paid and unskilled service jobs, employers have found that it is too expensive to expand and take on more workers, for service industries are labour-intensive and most of the costs of companies in this sector go on wages. As Dahrendorf recognises, 'In countries in which wages are notoriously "sticky" – as they are in much of Europe – services are expensive, indeed often too expensive to be available at all;

which means that some cannot find any jobs and remain unemployed' (Dahrendorf 1980: 12).

A second point he makes is that, because the underclass suffers from multiple disadvantages, no single policy initiative is likely to break the cycle of deprivation. It is not enough to generate jobs, he says, because the underclass may not be motivated to take them. Urban renewal improves the housing stock, but more often than not, it simply displaces the underclass elsewhere. Education and training schemes can play an important part, not only in equipping people for employment, but also in breaking what he calls a 'barrier of indolence', but Dahrendorf rejects policies which link payment of benefits to training or to work (as in the 'workfare' system introduced in a number of American states) on the grounds that they come 'dangerously close to forced labour' (Dahrendorf 1980: 14).

The proposal which Dahrendorf himself eventually comes up with is an expansion of local initiatives headed by community development workers who have the ability to lead depressed communities in new directions. This proposal, however, does not bear close scrutiny for it ignores the problem of dependency discussed above. It can be argued that the underclass is in part defined by the fact that it has other people doing things for it, in which case community development workers will become just one more set of agents of the state acting upon these people. An expansion of local initiatives would certainly benefit the social work profession, but it is doubtful whether it would benefit the underclass.

Any attempt to determine what 'should' be done will of course reflect the political values and beliefs of those making the proposal. In my view (for what it is worth) the challenge for social policy in the 1990s is to find ways of enabling the self-help of the underclass rather than offering yet more help from outside. The existence of the underclass today is an indictment of the failure of post-war social policy, and is evidence of the need for a radical re-think. In a sense, the underclass is unintentionally reproduced as a result of the existence of a vast welfare bureaucracy which caters to it. Neo-liberal writers such as Milton Friedman, recognising the paradox that state welfare contributes to the very problem it is intended to solve, argue that we should move away from policies which create dependency by stripping people of the ability or will to get off their knees. In their view, the solution lies in turning clients into customers by enabling people to buy what they want rather than providing them with what policy professionals believe they need. Friedman has suggested that this could be done by introducing a system of 'negative income tax' (in which people on low incomes receive 'tax' payments) supplemented by voucher schemes where appropriate (for example, vouchers to enable people to buy the kind of health insurance and education they want). In this way, the underclass could be *empowered* in that its members would enjoy the capacity to make choices and determine its own priorities. As the left sociologists of the 1960s recognised, the culture of poverty disappears very quickly when people find they can to some extent reclaim control over their own fate, thereby re-establishing a sense of self-worth and dignity.

Further reading

On the division of ownership and control and the rise of managerial capitalism, see Ralph Dahrendorf (1969) Class and Class Conflict in Industrial Society, *London: Routledge & Kegan Paul, ch. 2 and Theo Nichols (1969)* Ownership, Control and Ideology, *London: Allen & Unwin. The growth of the public sector middle class is discussed by R. Bacon and W. Eltis (1978)* Britain's Economic Problem: Too Few Producers, *London: Macmillan, and its political implications are discussed in Patrick Dunleavy and Christopher Husbands (1986)* Democracy at the Crossroads, *London: Allen & Unwin. This latter source is also a useful reference on the issue of class dealignment in voting; see also B. Sarlvik and I. Crewe (1979)* Decade of Dealignment, *Cambridge: Cambridge University Press, and A. Heath. R. Jowell and*

127

J. Curtice (1985) How Britain Votes, *Oxford: Pergamon Press. A useful collection of papers on variations within the working class can be found in Martin Bulmer (ed.) (1975)* Working Class Images of Society, *London: Routledge & Kegan Paul – this includes the original 1966 Lockwood paper as well as his reply to his critics.*

6

Conclusions

We have seen in this book that Britain is an unequal society. Inequalities of wealth are considerable, although the spread of home ownership means that two-thirds of the population now owns an asset of considerable value. Inequalities of income are significant, although tax and welfare policies do have a considerable effect in reducing the incomes of top earners and increasing the incomes of the poor.

These inequalities of wealth and income derive principally from people's different positions in property and labour markets. We have seen that one of the problems in a Marxist class analysis is that it focuses entirely on ownership and non-ownership of property and thus neglects the importance of divisions in the labour market between people who can command high incomes and others who cannot. For this reason, we have organised discussion in this book around a Weberian conception of stratification, particularly as it has been applied and developed in the work of sociologists like David Lockwood. Seen from this perspective, we have to understand people's positions in the stratification system, not only in terms of their material resources, but also in terms of their status situation and their political power (or lack of it).

Approaching the question in this way, we have considered five main social classes in contemporary British society, although we saw that one of them – the capitalist class – has all but disappeared as a distinct stratum. The salaried section of the middle class, by contrast, has been growing, as has the lower middle class, although the division between this latter stratum and the working class is often unclear at the margins. The working class itself has been shrinking, and its situation is also changing as a result of rising affluence and the introduction of new technology. Finally, a small underclass is anchored at the bottom of the social, economic and political hierarchy and is becoming marginalised as the rest of society shares to a greater or lesser extent in the growing prosperity of the country as a whole.

It is often thought that the British class system is closed and rigid, but we have seen that this is not the case. Apart from members of the underclass, social mobility up and down the full range of the class system is common. It is also often thought that class inequality is self-evidently a 'bad thing' and that government should act more positively to reduce the economic differences between the classes. Again, however, we have seen that such a view can be challenged, both on the grounds that inequality is the price to be paid for future growth from which all can benefit, and because moral and political philosophy shows us that 'social justice' has just as much to do with how people come by what they have got as with how much or how little they end up with.

In this book we have also considered the long-neglected 'functionalist theory of stratification'. We saw that, although many of the criticisms brought against this theory could be answered, it was not true that a system of stratification is the only way in which a society can ensure that key positions are filled and their responsibilities adequately discharged. The alternative is a society based on coercion. There is, we saw, a trade-off between freedom and equality. Although every society known to us has been unequal, there is no reason in principle why an egalitarian society could not be possible, but it would necessarily be a society in which the freedoms which we tend to take for granted would be massively curtailed.

The study of social stratification is central to the sociological enterprise, but it is also a highly charged and emotive topic to address. Feelings run high when considering issues of inequality and power, and most if not all the sociological literature in this field has been produced by people who have their own, strongly held, personal views. The challenge for sociology is to hold these views in check while openly and critically addressing the evidence and the arguments available to us. Not only is this possible; it is essential if sociology is to realise its promise as a discipline which can surprise us with its findings and challenge our prejudices with its arguments.

References

Althusser, L. (1971) 'Ideology and ideological state apparatuses', in L. Althusser (ed.) *Lenin and Philosophy and Other Essays*, London: New Left Books.

Atkinson, A. (1972) *Unequal Shares*, London: Allen Lane.

Bauer, P. (1978) *Class on the Brain*, London: Centre for Policy Studies.

Bell, D. (1974) *The Coming of Post-Industrial Society*, London: Heinemann.

Berger, P. (1987) *The Capitalist Revolution*, London: Wildwood House.

Bourdieu, P. and Passeron, J. (1977) *Reproduction in Education, Society and Culture*, London: Sage.

Braverman, H. (1974) *Labor and Monopoly Capital*, U.S.: Monthly Review Press.

Central Statistical Office (various years) *Social Trends*, London: HMSO.

Crompton, R. and Jones, G. (1984) *White Collar Proletariat*, London: Macmillan.

Dahrendorf, R. (1987) 'The erosion of citizenship and its consequences for us all', *New Statesman*, 12 June: 12–15.

132

Dale, A., Gilbert, G. and Arber, S. (1985) 'Integrating women into class theory', *Sociology* 19: 384–408.

Davis, K. (1966) 'Reply to Tumin', in R. Bendix and S. Lipset (eds) *Class, Status and Power*, London: Routledge & Kegan Paul (originally in *American Sociological Review* 18, 1953).

Davis, K. and Moore, W. (1966) 'Some principles of stratification', in R. Bendix and S. Lipset (eds), *Class, Status and Power*, London: Routledge & Kegan Paul (originally in *American Sociological Review* 10, 1945).

Diamond, Lord (1976) *Royal Commission on the Distribution of Income and Wealth*, London: HMSO.

Duke, V. and Edgell, S. (1984) 'Public expenditure cuts in Britain and consumption sectoral cleavages', *International Journal of Urban and Regional Research* 8: 177–201.

Dunleavy, P. (1979) 'The urban bases of political alignment', *British Journal of Political Science* 9: 409–43.

Durkheim, E. (1933) *The Division of Labour in Society*, London: Macmillan.

Friedman, M. (1962) *Capitalism and Freedom*, Chicago: University of Chicago Press.

Friedman, M. and Friedman, R. (1980) *Free to Choose*, London: Secker & Warburg.

Garrett, S. (1987) *Gender*, London: Tavistock.

Giddens, A. (1984) *The Constitution of Society*, Cambridge: Polity Press.

Goldthorpe, J. (1980) *Social Mobility and Class Structure in Modern Britain*, Oxford: Clarendon Press.

Goldthorpe, J., Lockwood, D., Bechhofer, F. and Platt, J. (1969) *The Affluent Worker in the Class Structure*, Cambridge: Cambridge University Press.

Goldthorpe, J. and Payne, C. (1986) 'Trends in intergenerational class mobility in England and Wales 1972–1983', *Sociology* 20: 1–24.

Gorz, A. *Farewell to the Working Class*, London: Pluto Press.

Habermas, J. (1976) *Legitimation Crisis*, London: Heinemann.

Hayek, F. (1960) *The Constitution of Liberty*, London: Routledge & Kegan Paul.

Heath, A., Jowell, R. and Curtice, J. (1985) *How Britain Votes*, Oxford: Pergamon Press.

Inkeles, A. and Rossi, P. (1956) 'National comparisons of occupational prestige', *American Journal of Sociology* 61: 329–39.

Lane, D. (1971) *The End of Inequality?* Harmondsworth: Penguin Books.

Lash, S. and Urry, J. (1987) *The End of Organised Capitalism*, Cambridge: Polity Press.

Lockwood, D. (1958) *The Blackcoated Worker*, London: Allen & Unwin.

————(1966) 'Sources of variation in working-class images of society', *Sociological Review* 14: 249–67.

Marcuse, H. (1964) *One-dimensional Man*, London: Routledge & Kegan Paul.

Marshall, G., Newby, H., Rose, D. and Vogler, C. (1988) *Social Class in Modern Britain*, London: Hutchinson.

Marshall, G., Vogler, C., Rose, D. and Newby, H. (1987) 'Distributional struggle and moral order in a market society', *Sociology* 21: 55–74.

Marx, K. (1970) 'Critique of the Gotha programme', in K. Marx and F. Engels, *Selected Works*, London: Lawrence & Wishart.

Marx, K. (1976) *Capital*, Harmondsworth: Penguin Books, vol. 1.

Merton, R. (1949) *Social Theory and Social Structure*, New York: Free Press.

Nozick, R. (1974) *Anarchy, State and Utopia*, Oxford: Basil Blackwell.

O'Donnell, M. (1985) *Age and Generation*, London: Tavistock.

Office of Population Censuses and Surveys (1980) *Classification of Occupations*, London: HMSO.

Orwell, G. (1945) *Animal Farm*, London: Secker & Warburg.

Pahl, R. (1984) *Divisions of Labour*, Oxford: Basil Blackwell.

————(1988) 'Some remarks on informal work, social polarization and the social structure', *International Journal of Urban and Regional Research*, 12: 247–67.

Parkin, F. (1979) *Marxism and Class Theory: a Bourgeois Critique*, London: Tavistock.

Poulantzas, N. (1975) *Classes in Contemporary Capitalism*, London: New Left Books.

Rawls, J. (1972) *A Theory of Justice*, Oxford: Oxford University Press.

Rex, J. and Tomlinson, S. (1979) *Colonial Immigrants in a British City*, London: Routledge & Kegan Paul.

Schumpeter, J. (1943) *Capitalism, Socialism and Democracy*, London: Allen & Unwin.

Sharpe, T. (1974) *Porterhouse Blue*, London: Secker & Warburg.

Townsend, P. (1979) *Poverty in the United Kingdom*, Harmondsworth: Penguin Books.

Tumin, M. (1966) 'Some principles of stratification: a critical analysis', in R. Bendix and S. Lipset (eds) *Class, Status and Power*, London: Routledge & Kegan Paul (originally published in *American Sociological Review* 18, 1953).

Weber, M. (1968) *Economy and Society*, New York: Bedminster Press.

Wright, E. (1978) *Class, Crisis and the State*, London: New Left Books.

Index

136

individuals 20; bias in law 45; consciousness 18, 19, 23; contradictory locations 16–17; dealignment 116, 127; fractions 15; fragmentation of 85–6, 123; interests 8; as market power 22, 25; openness of 68–9, 70, 72, 76, 77, 130; as ownership of means of production 6–9, 25, 129; pertinence of 12–15, 21, 23; polarisation 17–18, 86, 92; in socialist societies 55; struggle as motor of change 17; subjective aspects of 101, 108–10, 111, 113, 117; systems of classification 27–34, 75, 104–5, 118–19; *see also* false consciousness

clerks *see* white collar workers

closure 94

Cohen, G. 67

commercial classes 22, 29, 34

communism 46

community development 126

Conservative Party 107, 112, 116

consumerism 18, 111, 115

Crewe, I. 127

Crompton, R. 100–2, 103, 104

Cuba 56

cultural capital 77, 111

Dahrendorf, R. 121–3, 125, 127

Dale, A. 118

Davis, K. 57–64, 68

deferential workers 108–9

democracy 55

dependency 123, 125, 126

deskilling 31, 99–102, 114

difference principle 47–8

Director's Law 39

discrimination 13; positive 44

Douglas, J. 27

Duke, V. 116

Dunleavy, P. 96, 116, 127

Durkheim, E. 72–3, 83

education, as basis of class membership 22–3, 76, 93, 96–7; expansion of 69, 95; training 58, 63–4, 94, 97, 126; as transmitter of ideology 9, 18–19; use by different classes 39, 42

Edgell, S. 116

elites 2, 13, 88

Eltis, W. 127

embourgeoisement 31, 107, 109–14, 116–17

Engels, F. 9, 18, 26

equality, antithetical to liberty 67, 131; legal 43, 44, 45, 47; of opportunity 43, 46, 77, 81; of outcome 44, 46, 65–7

estate duties 34–5

estates system 12, 43

ethnicity 2, 3, 13–14, 21, 42, 44, 77, 120–1

exploitation 6, 7–10, 18, 19, 45, 90

expropriation 50

false consciousness 9, 18–19, 23

fatalism 124, 125

feudalism 5, 9, 12, 50, 60, 68

financial institutions 18, 86, 89–90, 95

France 12, 15

Friedman, M. 66, 123, 127

functionalist theory of stratification 56–67, 130–1

Garrett, S. 2

gender 2, 11, 12–13, 14, 21, 42, 44, 77, 98, 102–4, 118

Giddens, A. 12, 25

Gilbert, G. 118

Goldthorpe, J. 31, 32–4, 40, 74–8, 80–83, 110–12, 114, 116, 118

Gorz, A. 113

Gramsci, A. 9

Green, D. 67